Moreton Morrell Site

Contents

£15.00
936.
1
IAR
D23)

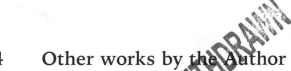

Cover photographs: Neolithic pottery vessels, reconstruction of Roman fort gate, trilithon at Stonehenge, fine glassware from the Roman period, detail from a Roman mosaic floor, reconstruction of Iron Age round house, reconstruction of Iron Age chariot burial.

Editor
Greg Payne

Design Editor
Liz Wright

Origination
Sally Robinson

Published by
Greenlight Publishing
The Publishing House, 119 Newland Street
Witham, Essex CM8 1WF
Tel: 01376 521900   **Fax:** 01376 521901
mail@greenlightpublishing.co.uk
www.greenlightpublishing.co.uk

Printed in Great Britain

ISBN 1 897738 137
© 2003 Greenlight Publishing

Other Works By The Author

Discovering Regional Archaeology series:

Central England (1970)
North West England (1971)
North East England (1971)

The Early Barrow Diggers (1974)
The Burial Mounds of Derbyshire (1977)
Discovering Roman Britain (co-author 1983)
Chesterfield Trams and Trolleybuses (1984)
Pioneers of Prehistory (1984)
A Few of the Derbyshire 'Few' (1987)
Tramtracks and Trolleybooms (1988)
The Barrow Knight (1988)
Glossop Tramways (1991)
The Early Barrow Diggers (revised and enlarged 1999)
A Chesterfield Tramscape (2001)
Ilkeston Tramways (2002)
North Derbyshire Tramways (2002)
Chesterfield Trolley buses (2002)

For Children

Prehistoric Britain (1989)
Roman Invaders and Settlers (1992)

Introduction

The 19th century antiquary John Thurnam (1810-1873) spoke of archaeology as "healthful recreation, suited to our taste" while his contemporary Thomas Bateman (1821-1861) regarded "these journeys in search of the antique" as "affording the happiest portion of his career." This book is intended to assist all enthusiasts who wish to seek out English field monuments for themselves, together with information on the artefacts of the periods discussed in the work, and guidance on museums containing material from the Prehistoric and Roman eras.

Landscapes have, of course, changed immeasurably between now and the time the sites were in use, and imagination has to supply the details now lacking. Nevertheless, a variety of earthworks and other structures still survive in the English landscape, and visits to locate them, followed by time spent in appropriate museums will help aficionados to relate excavated objects to their sources, and place tools, weapons, pottery, and religious and decorative items in their proper context.

Most sites are easy of access, although those on private land require the granting of permission to visit them as a matter of courtesy. This guide caters primarily for the amateur travelling by car, but a detailed examination of a locality can only really be achieved by an exploration on foot. Maps are, of course, essential for finding sites, and either the 1:50,000 Landranger or 1:25,000 Pathfinder Ordnance Survey maps are more than adequate for searchers. The first shows both rights of way and public footpaths. It only remains to wish the enthusiast good weather and good hunting in their own "search of the antique."

Barry M. Marsden
Eldwick, March 2003

The Palaeolithic & Mesolithic Ages

Early humans roamed over Western Europe from the time Britain was still joined to the Continent. Their progress across England was limited during certain periods by the spread of glacial ice sheets, which at their furthest southern extent reached as far as the Thames valley.

During the warmer periods between the Ice Ages, the so-called "interglacials", the climate was warm enough for oak forests to spread over the fertile parts of the country, promoting the extension of animal species northwards, followed by man who hunted them for food and clothing.

Human presence is indicated by the finding of stone tools, weapons and working floors, and the rare recovery of fossilised bones. Large numbers of stone tools have been uncovered in England, but very few have been uncovered in working and living areas; lacking significant find spots, these examples are only useful as specimens. Traces of mobile hunter-gatherers are mostly found in the open country, on areas of hilltop gravel, or on the banks of ancient rivers. Very few vestiges of such sites remain, though at Swanscombe in Kent the find-spot of a human skull some 350,000 years old is now a protected site.

Although such localities lack appeal, of more interest are the remains located in rock shelters and caves. It must be stressed that few of these early groups lived in caves or other shelters, and such places may have become much altered since they provided refuges. In any case, the living area was usually the cave mouth and entrance, the interiors being dark and moist, and occasionally the habitat of the ferocious cave bear (Fig.1.).

Fig.1. Skulls of the savage cave bear in Skipton Museum, North Yorkshire. These formidable beasts vied with early humans for the possession of caverns during the last Ice Age.

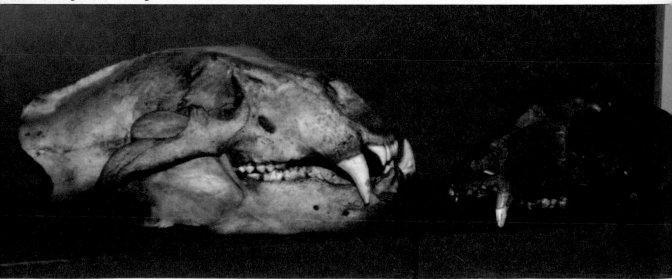

Fig.2. Plan of the Creswell Crags ravine in North Derbyshire, a classic site of the last Ice Age in Britain. The main caves are named, and the two magnesian limestone rock faces are riddled with some 20 caverns and shelters.

Fig.3. The Pin Hole during an early excavation in the 1870s. The contents of the cave were literally shovelled out, and much valuable information on the site was lost forever.

No English caves have produced examples of painted art, although a few have yielded carved bone, tooth or antler ornaments. Several inhabited caverns are open to the public; they include the Creswell Crags complex in North Derbyshire (Figs.2&3.) Here a magnesian limestone ravine is cut by a small stream, and its two rock faces are riddled with a series of caves and rock shelters (Fig.4.). The larger of these sites was seasonally occupied by hunter-fisher communities of the late Palaeolithic period, although there was earlier sparse habitation by Neanderthals. The earliest tenure was circa 43,000 BC, then 30-28,000 BC, and finally around 10,000 BC. Traces of later occupation have also been found down to Roman and later times.

Fig.4. An aerial view of the ravine from the south. The Pin Hole is centre left, and the lake on the right is a comparatively recent feature. Animal herds roaming the gorge were comparatively easy prey for the hunters who lived here during the arctic summers.

Fig.5. Robin Hood's Cave is an extensive system, with two entrances. Homo Sapien hunters lived in the cave entrances, and did not penetrate any distance inside. Large numbers of animal bones were recovered from the cave during digs in the 1870s.

Fig.6. *The Pin Hole gets its name from its narrow, diminishing length. It was the earliest of the caves at Creswell to be inhabited, by bands of Neanderthals, from around 45,000BC.*

Fig.7. *Another rival to humans for cave occupation was the hyena. Judging by the remains found at Creswell, these scavengers existed in considerable numbers in the locality.*

Fig.8. *The early humans who seasonally occupied the Creswell caves were superb craftsmen in flint, bone and antler. This splendid bone pin was found in Church Hole cave.*

Fig.9. *Found in Robin Hood's Cave, this horse's head incised on a piece of reindeer rib is one of the rare examples of representational art found in Ice Age Britain.*

A Visitor Centre explains the site, and guided tours of certain caves are available if pre-booked. The main sites are north of the B6042, which presently runs through the gorge. From east to west they include Mother Grundy's Parlour, a horseshoe shaped cavern with a cramped passage leading off north-east. Numerous poorly-documented finds include flints and split bones. Robin Hood's Cave (Fig.5.) has two entrances leading to two main chambers. Many fine flint tools have been found here, plus a carving of a horse's head on a reindeer rib and the bones of many extinct animal species, including the woolly rhinoceros. The Pin Hole (Fig.6.) is a narrow diminishing cave 15m long, occupied by Neanderthals and later used by hyenas (Fig.7.). Finds have been made of decorated bones including one doubtful specimen engraved with a human figure.

On the south side of the stream is Church Hole, a straight cave 60m long and lived in until Roman times. Finds here included a superb bone pin (Fig.8.). Most of the material from Creswell was passed on to Manchester Museum, where displays of some of it can be seen, although the incised horse's head (Fig.9.) is in the British Museum. Other material from Creswell consists of Neanderthal type hand axes made from pebbles found in the nearby stream (Fig.10.), and deer ribs embellished with designs carved with flint burins (Fig.11.). Flakes were struck off prepared cores as seen in Fig.12., which also shows the bone tools used in the striking.

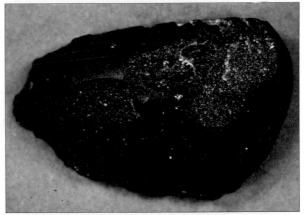

Fig.10. *Hand axes are ubiquitous tools found all over the Palaeolithic world. This example is of Neanderthal design, and was made from a Bunter pebble taken from the stream at Creswell.*

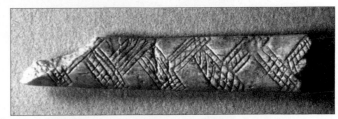

Fig.11. *This strip of deer rib was carved with a geometric design made with a sharp flint graving tool or burin.*

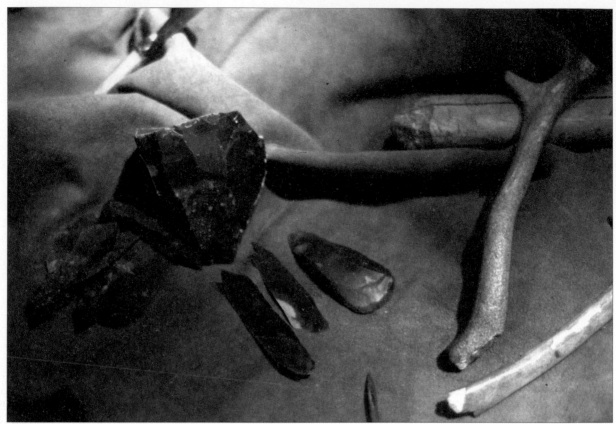

Fig.12. The flint core in the centre of the illustration had prepared flakes struck off it using the bone and antler tools placed alongside. The struck flakes can be seen around the core. They were turned into knives, scrapers, spearheads and other implements.

Fig.13. Typical flint blades from "Creswellian" sites such as Cheddar, and used for a variety of purposes such as blades, gravers and burins.

Kent's Cavern, Torquay, now a show cave, was occupied by Palaeolithic hunters who left flint hand axes and laurel-leaf blades, as well as smaller blades similar to those found at Creswell. A few bone and antler tools have also been unearthed here. A piece of human mandible, carbon-dated to 30,000 BC, is the earliest evidence of modern man found in Britain. Profuse remains of Pleistocene animals have also been uncovered, many of which can be seen in the local museum at the resort.

The Cheddar Gorge contains a number of caves and fissures, the most famous being the Gough's Cave show cave. This site was inhabited between 12,000-8,000 BC, and recent excavations have revealed evidence of extensive hunting and processing of meat from the red deer and horse. Broken-up human bones, which suggested the cutting off of the meat and smashing for marrow extraction, hint at cannibalistic practices. Several thousand flint artefacts, mostly blades (Fig.13.), have also been unearthed here, plus a few carved bones. The latter includes two perforated batons, one made out of the humerus from a human arm. Finds can be seen in the Cheddar Caves Museum, together with animal bones from the same period, and the skeleton of the so-called "Cheddar Man", which is dated to very late in this period (around 7130 BC). Smaller sites include Flint Jack's Cave, Soldier's Hole, and Sun Hole, also lived in during the same time span as Gough's Cave.

On the northern edge of Langcliffe Scar, above Settle in North Yorkshire, is Victoria Cave, the most northerly English cavern inhabited at the end of the last Ice Age, and lying very close to the permanent ice sheets just to the north. Above the remains of hippopotamus, woolly rhino, hyena and elephant, were bear, fox and red deer bones, mixed with tools of the period, including harpoon points made from antler and red deer bone. Some of the finds from the cave are in Skipton Museum.

Between 12,000 and 4,000 BC the English climate gradually warmed up and small groups of food-gatherers, fishermen and hunters spread across the countryside. Around 8,000 BC the sea level had risen as a result of the melting of the ice, and had flooded the area now known as the North Sea. As a result Britain had become an island. The Mesolithic era, covering the period from around 10,000-4,200 BC, represented a transition from the wandering to a more settled way of life. On the coastal sites, groups of travellers collected shellfish, whose empty shells and other debris were left in large middens (Fig.14.).

Small and scattered transitory settlements still existed, usually on the higher ground, and on the lighter soils, such as a site at Abinger in Surrey where a primitive shelter may have existed, associated with several thousand microlithic flint tools, and a nearby water supply. The most famous Mesolithic camping site in England, Starr Carr near

Fig.14. Shell middens, such as the one illustrated, were formed by the hunter-gatherers of the early Mesolithic period, who collected the shellfish for food and dumped the waste product in often large piles that accumulated over time.

Scarborough, has nothing now left to see, although this organic platform, built on the edge of a glacial lake, housed several hunting and fishing families on a seasonal basis. The site has produced a wealth of finds including numbers of antler spears and harpoons (Fig.15.), bone mattocks (Fig.16.) flint axes, and red deer antler frontlets, the latter used as headdresses, either for rituals or as disguises in hunting forays. The most common remains from this period are the tiny flint microliths used as hunting equipment in composite bows, spears or harpoons. There were some attempts at landscape management during this time, using stone axes for forest clearance.

Fig.15. *Mesolithic spear and harpoon blades fashioned from deer antler; these were used to spear fish and hunt animals. The hole in one example is presumably for the weapon to be retrieved using a length of cord tied to it.*

Fig.16. *Bone mattocks from Star Carr. These were used to grub up roots and other vegetable foodstuffs. The specimen on the right still has part of the wooden handle preserved in the hole.*

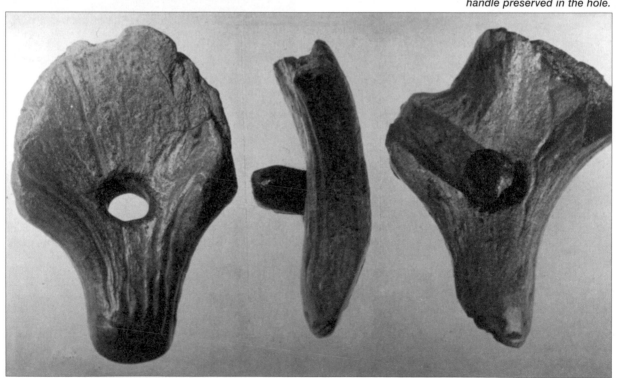

The Neolithic Age

Fig.17. A range of Neolithic pottery vessels, mostly round-based. On the left are early thick-walled cooking pots. The decorated one in the centre is of Mortlake style. On the right is a flat-bottomed grooved ware vessel, named after the incised ornamentation.

The original inhabitants of England had begun the transition from hunter-gathering to simple agriculture from about 4500 BC. Domesticated kinds of plants and animals began arriving from Europe by one means or another, and the development of specialised types of stone axes made it easier to clear woodland. These clearings allowed for crop growing and the breeding of animals.

The manufacture of the first pottery in the country, plain, round-based vessels (Figs.17-19.) indicates a more settled lifestyle, despite the difficulties in locating the transient homes of the inhabitants. During this period (between 4200-2200 BC), the native population began constructing field monuments, and dug deep pits for the large-scale exploitation of flint. The earliest field monuments were the causewayed enclosures, which so far have not been traced north of the English midlands, although they surely must have existed beyond this boundary. They consist of concentric rings of interrupted ditches, ranging from one to three in number, with un-dug stretches between the ditches (the causeways), and earth banks on their inner sides. There are no obvious entrances, and little evidence of structures inside. Any domestic rubbish is found in the infill of the inner ditches, and consists of pottery

Fig.18. An early crude round-bottomed pot placed as an offering in a long barrow of the period.

shards, stone axes and other tools, with animal and human bone seemingly deliberately buried, sometimes in the form of skeletons. These puzzling enclosures apparently had a variety of uses, including regional centres for trade and exchange of goods. Some seem to have been built for settlement, as at Knap Hill, Wiltshire (Fig.20.), although permanent buildings are lacking; others appear to be refuges for use in time of danger, and a number of these provide archaeological evidence for attacks and storming.

Crickley Hill, five miles from Gloucester in a country park part-owned by the National Trust, began as a causewayed enclosure around 3,000 BC, and was presumably built for defence. It was later attacked and burned, with many scattered flint leaf-shaped arrowheads attesting to the fierceness of the assault. At some time late during the Neolithic occupation a small shrine was established at the western end of the eminence, later covered by a long mound of rubble and a small stone ring, with a central burning slab.

Fig.19. *A Mortlake style pot decorated with bird bone impressions, and found with burials in a Derbyshire rock-shelter. On the right is an accompanying flint arrowhead.*

Fig.20. *The single line of interrupted ditches at the Knap Hill causewayed enclosure can be clearly seen as they form a ring around the upper part of the eminence.*

Hambledon Hill, near Child Okeford in Dorset, also began as two causewayed enclosures; the smaller one on Stepleton spur was perhaps a settlement. The larger site, north-west of this, was a single ring of ditches which were filled with human bones, with skulls laid on the ditch bottoms and offerings of pottery and stone axes in pits dug into the bases of the ditches. This monument was obviously a mortuary site, with corpses probably exposed for de-fleshing in the central area. The most famous of all causewayed "camps" is Windmill Hill, north-west of Avebury in Wiltshire; it is the largest and the easiest to access (Fig.21.). The inner ditch has a diameter of 360m, and the total area of the earthwork is 8.5h.

Excavations have produced some of the earliest pottery found in Britain, all round-based and baggy in shape (Fig.22.). Settlement existed on the hill from 3,700 BC, but the ditches and banks appeared

some 400 years later. As well as occupation evidence, the site appears to have functioned as a trading centre for the exchange of pots, stone axes, and other wares. Animal bones suggest herding and slaughtering for food or ritual purposes, and human burials - including those of children - have been uncovered in the ditch bottoms (Fig.23.). All the finds from Windmill Hill are to be seen in the superb little museum in nearby Avebury.

Long barrows came into use at the end of the 4th millennium BC, and were of two types. The earliest were the earthen ones, oblong or wedge-shaped mounds broader and higher at one end, and these are found mainly in the south-west, an area designated Wessex by archaeologists. It consists of Wiltshire, Dorset and the adjoining counties, where prehistoric

Fig.21. The triple circle of concentric ditches at Windmill Hill. Note the small square contemporary enclosure at bottom left, and the later early Bronze Age round barrows. The example at the top right has had its surrounding ditch cleared out.

Fig.22. Typical of the pottery found at Windmill Hill are these thick, baggy vessels. The one on the left has a set of carrying handles.

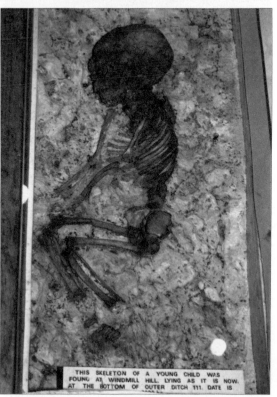

Fig.23. Several human skeletons were buried in the ditches at Windmill Hill, including this infant, displayed in the floor at Avebury Museum.

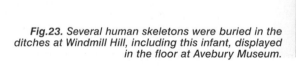

THIS SKELETON OF A YOUNG CHILD WAS FOUND AT WINDMILL HILL, LYING AS IT IS NOW, AT THE BOTTOM OF OUTER DITCH 111. DATE IS

Fig.24. The Wor Barrow on Cranborne Chase, Dorset, dug by General Pitt Rivers in the 1890s. He had the ditches cleared out to check the volume of material they contained. The barrow mound is on the right.

Fig.25. The collective remains of some 15 individuals placed in a timber mortuary house under a long barrow at Whitwell, Derbyshire. Note their weathered condition, suggesting exposure or pre-burial elsewhere before their removal to the site.

monuments are common. They also occur in East Anglia, and on the Lincolnshire and Yorkshire Wolds.

These mounds were usually built up using soil from flanking ditches (Fig.24.), heaped up over a turf or timber mortuary house at the higher end, and normally provided with access via an entrance. The sides of the mounds were usually revetted with upright posts or strong lateral fencing. The mortuary building contained collective human burials (Fig.25.), which were often exposed elsewhere to allow the flesh to decay, before they were removed to the barrow. The mounds were usually impressive in size, and were often sited on high points to emphasise the cult of the ancestors who were interred there. Ceremonies took place at the barrows from time to time, and bones were frequently removed or transferred, indicating that the burial mounds were houses for the dead that were re-entered on special occasions, rather than burial places in the strictest sense. The

Fig.26. *The Pimperne Long Barrow is the biggest in England. It has never been excavated, and the flanking ditches are still clearly visible. The mound is 105m long, 30m wide and 2.5m high.*

Fig.27. *Many chambered barrows in Wessex have forecourts set between dry-walled "horns" in front of the burial chambers, as in this example at Lanhill in Wiltshire. Ceremonies connected with the dead are believed to have taken place in these sacred areas.*

largest surviving earthen long barrow is at Pimperne in Dorset (Fig.26.). Most of these monuments have been badly damaged over the course of time, and few are worth visiting. Finds are rare, and the only artefacts placed with the bones were pots, animal bones and, very rarely, flints.

Chambered barrows are believed to be slightly later than the earliest earthen mounds, and are quite widely distributed in England. They can be seen in the south-west, Kent, the Peak District, and are scattered in smaller numbers on the periphery of these localities. Some of the retaining mounds are round or ovoid, rather than long, and some were reshaped, rebuilt or added to over time. They were revetted by upright stones, or dry walling, or a combination of both, and contained stone built chambers, often connected by a passage to the outside, which often had a forecourt (Fig.27.) for ceremonies at the front end.

Fig.28. A long barrow vault recreated at Woodstock Museum in Oxfordshire, showing the remains of several interments from a local site, scattered across a paved floor.

2 Crania from the Dinnington Barrow

Fig.29. Typical longheaded Neolithic skulls from a destroyed long barrow at Wath in South Yorkshire and now displayed in Rotherham Museum.

Fig.30. Another distinctive skull with the same racial characteristics. This came from the Five Wells cairn, near Taddington in Derbyshire.

Fig.31. One of the finest restored chambered long barrows is West Kennet, near Avebury in Wiltshire. The view shows the rebuilt façade of upright sarsen stones placed across the entrance to the barrow when it was finally closed during the 2nd millennium BC.

Some examples have access from the exterior via chambers built in the sides, whilst others have chambers sealed inaccessibly within the structure. Being durably constructed, they were in use for up to a millennium, and bones were frequently added or abstracted over time, the rites being the same as those observed in the earthen mounds. The remains of men, women and children are found in the vaults (Fig.28.), suggesting equal access for perhaps the families of the ruling elite. As in the earthen long barrows, the skulls are of the *dolichocephalic* or long-headed variety, a distinct racial type in contrast to the later *brachycephalic* or round-headed form of cranium, which appears in the Early Bronze Age (Figs.29&30..) In many areas the mounds covering the chambers have disappeared, leaving only the stones forming the vaults, or remnants of them.

Among the best preserved of the chambered long barrows are West Kennet (Fig.31.), near Avebury in Wiltshire, and Stoney Littleton (Fig.32.) near Wellow in Somerset. Both covering mounds have been restored and it is possible to walk inside them and view the chambers leading off on both sides. The five chambers at the former enclosed a total of 46 burials, discovered by modern excavators.

Fig.32. The entrance to the Stoney Littleton Long Barrow, showing the dry-walled horns forming the forecourt. The side entrance slab at the lower left has a fossil ammonite preserved in it. The barrow boasts three pairs of side chambers, and an end chamber, but has been long rifled.

Fig.33. The rebuilt façade at Wayland's Smithy on the Oxfordshire Ridgeway. This impressive chambered mound was raised over an earlier earthen long barrow, preserving the continuity of the doubtless sacred locality. Note the dry-walling between the upright sarsens.

Fig.34. The imposing blind entrance to the now-vanished Kits Coty House in Kent. There would once have been a substantial long mound behind the remaining stonework.

Belas Knap, near Charlton Abbots in Gloucestershire has a blind entrance at the front, perhaps ritual in purpose, set between a pair of dry-walled "horns" forming a forecourt as at Stoney Littleton, and the burial chambers are set down the sides and back end of the mound.

Hetty Pegler's Tump, near Uley in the same county also retains its covering mound and capstones, while the Notgrove long barrow - although denuded of its soil - is well worth a visit.

Other long barrows, which should be seen in the south, include Wayland's Smithy (Fig.33.), on the prehistoric track known as the Ridgeway near Ashbury in Oxfordshire. On this site a chambered long barrow overlies an earlier earthen one.

In Kent there are the remnants of several badly damaged chambered barrows, but Kit's Coty House near Aylesford (Fig.34.) is a fine example of a blind entrance at the front of a completely destroyed mound.

The remains of other stone chambers such as the Devil's Den near Marlborough in Wiltshire (Fig.35.) are scattered across the English countryside, and can be located by using the gazetteers listed in the bibliography. Some chamber entrances have "porthole" access as at the Gatcombe long barrow in Gloucestershire (Fig.36.). There are good reconstructions of long barrow chambers and their contents in the museums at Woodstock in Oxfordshire, and Cirencester in Gloucestershire (Fig.37.).

Fig.35. Sometimes only the bare chamber stones of a destroyed long barrow are left to see, as at the splendidly named Devil's Den, near Marlborough in Wiltshire.

Fig.36. Some chamber entrances are part-blocked by "portholes" as in this Gloucestershire example. Bones were passed through this narrow hole, which was blocked off with dry-stone walling between burial ceremonies.

Fig.37. Another reconstructed Neolithic burial chamber from the Hazelton long barrow, as seen at Cirencester Museum in Gloucestershire.

Several sites in the Derbyshire Peak are well worth a visit. Minning Low, standing on a prominent hill near Ballidon is an oval cairn with several visible chambers, two still retaining their capstones (Fig.38.). Excavations have shown that this barrow was expanded several times to include fresh vaults.

Five Wells, near Taddington, consists of two back-to-back chambers, with two approach passages (Fig.39.), and is the highest chambered cairn in England. Just across the border in Staffordshire is Long Low, near Wetton, which is a bank barrow, similar in plan to sites in North Yorkshire and Wiltshire. It consists of two mounds linked together by a low bank. The north-eastern cairn covered a large vault containing some 13 disarticulated skeletons. There are a few chambered barrows in Yorkshire, including Hedon Howe, excavated in the 1890s, and disclosing similar collective burial rites as those in other parts of England (Fig.40.).

Finds in Neolithic barrows are rare, and consist mainly of simple pottery, much of it round-bottomed, plus animal bones presumably left as food for the deceased, and flints. The latter are mainly leaf-shaped arrowheads often of great beauty and obviously specially made for the use of the dead in afterlife. As these tombs went out of use, they were sealed off: the earthen ones by palisades of heavy timbers, the chambered examples by facades of upright slabs, such as the one to be seen at West Kennett.

Occasionally, as a funerary ritual, the wooden mortuary chambers of the former barrows were set on fire and burned out. In parts of England burials were sometimes placed in caves or rock shelters. Examples of this type of interment, in two Derbyshire sites, are shown in Figs.41 and 42.

Fig.38. Two limestone burial vaults at Minning Low still retain their cover stones. This is Chamber 1 at the centre of the huge cairn. Though badly disturbed by stone-wallers, the entrance passage can be seen at the bottom right.

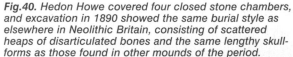

Fig.39. Impressively sited at 425m above sea level, Five Wells contains two back-to-back chambers. The capstones are missing, but the pair of fine portal pillars still survive intact.

Fig.40. Hedon Howe covered four closed stone chambers, and excavation in 1890 showed the same burial style as elsewhere in Neolithic Britain, consisting of scattered heaps of disarticulated bones and the same lengthy skull-forms as those found in other mounds of the period.

Fig.41. Occasionally in the Neolithic era burials were made in rock clefts or shelters. Here at Demon's Dale, near Taddington, a series of skeletons were placed at intervals in a deep shaft. Note how a later interment has partly displaced an earlier one.

Fig.42. In a side valley off Monsal Dale, Derbyshire, a crouched burial has been laid in a cist. A bundle of ribs from another interment lie in front of the face, while the sacrum has been placed against the rock in front of the knees. Note also the two child's lower jaws between the ribs and sacrum, and the long-headed cranium of the burial.

Another type of earthwork that had its origins in Neolithic times is the cursus, a long and narrow ceremonial enclosure marked by parallel ditches, high internal banks, and squared-off ends. Examples vary in length from 10km long and 80m wide, to much smaller examples less than 100m long and 5m wide, and they are invariably found near long barrows. They can be straight, like the Findern Cursus in South Derbyshire or the Stonehenge Cursus, or they can meander across long distances, like the Dorset Cursus on Cranborne Chase.

In North Yorkshire the Thornborough Cursus lies under a later henge, proving that these earthworks predate the latter. Several cursuses converge on the 7.7m high monolith at Rudston in North Yorkshire (Fig.43.), obviously the components of an important cult centre; however, they are largely ploughed out, and are only visible on aerial photographs. Their purpose is uncertain, although they may have functioned as enclosures for the spirits of the deceased. They appear to be part of the Neolithic ritual landscape of the departed, and even when they fell out of use their sacredness continued to be acknowledged, as can be demonstrated by the clusters of later Early Bronze Age barrows that surround them, like the ones alongside the Dorset Cursus.

The first henges appeared in England around 3,200 BC, and may have supplanted the older

Fig.43. The monolith in Rudston churchyard is, at nearly 8m high, the tallest in Britain. Set on a hill, it was the target for several cursuses, which are aimed directly at the pillar. This huge gritstone block was brought all the way from Cayton Bay, on the Yorkshire coast.

Fig.44. The Bull Ring henge monument near Buxton still retains its bank and ditch, and two opposed entrances, though the stone circle once existing on the inner lip of the ditch has long since been destroyed.

Fig.45. *Avebury in Wiltshire still retains some of the outer ring of massive sarsen stones on the inner edge of the massive ditch, and the remnants of the two inner circles, which can be seen centre and right.*

causewayed enclosures. They are found in most areas of the country where Neolithic settlement occurred, and consist of a circular and level central area ringed by a ditch and outer bank, with usually one or two opposed entrances. There are exceptions to this rule; in northern and eastern England some henges, like the three at Thornborough, have two ditches, whilst Mayburgh in Cumbria has none. There are great variations in size, from some 75m like the Bull Ring in Derbyshire (Fig.44.), to 450m at

Fig.46. *Arbor Low, near Bakewell, consists of an outer bank, inner ditch, and a ring of thrown down limestone slabs which once stood upright. Note the two opposite entrances, and the later round cairn on the left, added to the circle at a later date. The crater on its summit is the result of a 19th century dig.*

Durrington Walls in Wiltshire. Most henges are low-lying, and many are close to rivers. Excavations have revealed that few henges contain domestic rubbish, so they may have functioned as meeting places or ceremonial centres, with the populace watching ceremonies of one sort or another from the tops of the high banks. A number of henges, like Avebury (Fig.45) and Stonehenge in Wiltshire, Arbor Low in Derbyshire (Fig.46.), and Arminghall in Norfolk, contained inner circles of stone or wooden posts. Very large "super henges" include Durrington Walls and Marden in Wiltshire, and Mount Pleasant in Dorset.

Fig.47. A modern village stands inside the huge Avebury henge. Note the ditch, still deep despite centuries of natural infill, and the impressive bank built out of material from the former.

Stonehenge began life as a henge consisting of a double-ditch and bank, constructed around 3,000 BC, and perhaps a large round wooden building 30m in diameter at the centre of the enclosure. Many other henges still exist, including Avebury, so large that a village stands inside it (Fig.47.). Avebury boasts four entrances, and a ring of some 100 large

Fig.48. The central plateau of Avebury was once ringed with 100 large sarsens. Many fallen or buried ones have been set upright, and any gaps in the circle have been replaced with concrete posts like the one seen on the right.

Fig.49. The Kennet Avenue of paired stones runs south-east from the southern entrance of the henge to a smaller stone circle called the Sanctuary on Overton Hill; this was perhaps a meeting place for processions heading for the sacred site.

stones once stood along the lip of the central plateau (Fig.48.), with two inner circles side-by-side inside the outer circle. Two avenues of paired stones ran from the monument: the Kennet Avenue (Fig.49.) from the southern entrance to another set of stone rings called the Sanctuary on nearby Overton Hill, and the Beckhampton Avenue that ran from the western entrance; the terminus of this ruined route-way has not been established.

Also associated with Avebury is the huge four-phase monument known as Silbury Hill (Fig.50), a vast heap south of the henge, and dug into several times in the past. Raised by an immense effort of labour, the giant pile may be the burial mound of the builder of Avebury, although no burial has yet been located.

Fig.50. Silbury Hill, just south of Avebury still stands 40m high, and covers 2h. This mound, the largest Prehistoric monument of its kind in Europe, may cover the burial of the chieftain who built Avebury.

Fig.51. Arbor Low enjoys distant views, particularly to the north. The stones of the circle still exist, though they have been clearly pushed over. The bases of broken-off ones still project from the ground, and one on the left of the photograph still stands at a shallow angle.

Fig.52. Taken from the top of the later round cairn, the bank, ditch and central plateau of Arbor Low are clearly visible. Note the remains of the cove at the centre of the site.

Fig.53. The three Devil's Arrows, at Boroughbridge, North Yorkshire, are the remnants of a stone avenue, which is part of a ritual landscape and includes a number of henges. The southern example, shown here, is the tallest at nearly 7m. The flutings down the side are caused by natural weathering.

Other henges worth seeing include Arbor Low near Middleton by Youlgrave in Derbyshire, where the stone ring still exists (Fig.51.), although the stones have long been dismantled (Fig.52.). The Bull Ring, near Buxton, retains its bank and ditch, though here the stones have gone. At Knowlton in Dorset, a ruined church still stands within the monument, in an apparent attempt to Christianise a pagan site.

There are no less than three henges in a north-west to south-east line at Thornborough in North Yorkshire, although only the most northerly is rea-sonably intact, as it is covered by a copse of trees. The other two henges have been damaged by plough-ing, although their main features can still be seen.

A few miles away at Boroughbridge, the three standing stones known as the Devil's Arrows (Fig.53.) may well have been part of the Neolithic rit-ual landscape between the rivers Ure and Swale. In Cumbria, King Arthur's Round Table and Mayburgh, both at Eamont Bridge, still retain their banks, although the former earthwork has suffered damage in the past.

Fig.54.

Fig.55.

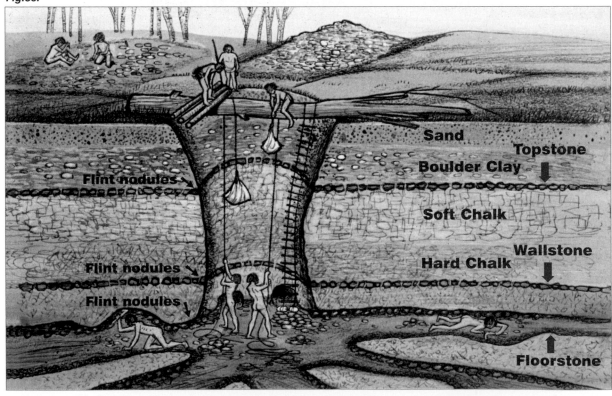

Sand

Topstone

Boulder Clay

Flint nodules

Soft Chalk

Flint nodules

Hard Chalk

Wallstone

Flint nodules

Floorstone

32

Fig.56.

During that period there was obviously a need for high quality stone and flint for the tools required for clearance, carpentry and hunting. Axe factories in Cumbria, North Wales and Devon produced fine-grained igneous rock for axes, while in the south and east flint provided the raw materials for arrowheads, knives, scrapers, axes and other tools (Fig.54.).

The best quality flint was found in seams deep in the chalk, and shafts were often dug for its extraction (Fig.55.). Mining areas can be seen at a number of sites, including Harrow Hill and the Cissbury hillfort in Sussex. In Norfolk a thriving flint industry grew up at Grimes Graves near Weeting, where nearly 500 deep shafts attest to the longevity of mining operations here. It is possible to descend one of the shafts, and appreciate the conditions under which the miners worked (Fig.56.), using deer antler picks and bone shovels to extract the raw flint (Figs.57&58.). A diminutive chalk-carved Buddha-like figurine claimed as found in one of the shafts during excavations in the 1920s, is now felt to be a fake (Fig.59.). It is thought that some 20,000 flint axes could have been fashioned each year at this site during the 3rd millennium BC.

At the end of the Neolithic era chambered barrows gradually went out of use, although in North Yorkshire huge round shaped mounds replaced them. Two of these giants are Duggleby Howe (Fig.60.), originally 9m high, and Willy Howe, near

Fig.54. A variety of flint tools, including a Palaeolithic hand axe (on the left), and a cleaver of similar age (lower right). The white flint axe is a product of the Neolithic mining industry, and the fine grained black polished axe comes from one of the scree-slope "factories" in Cumbria, North Wales or Devon, who supplied them by a process of trade.

Fig.55. Section through a flint mine, showing the access pit and radiating galleries. Flint occurs in seams in the chalk, and the best quality is the "floorstone" variety, at the third seam level. Note the flint knappers making tools at the top left of the picture.

Fig.56. The base of one of the mineshafts, showing the galleries dug out in the search for flint. They used chalk lamps whose brightness was enhanced by the white colour of the tunnel sides and roofs. A layer of "wallstone" flint can be seen in the walls of the shaft, above the gallery entrances.

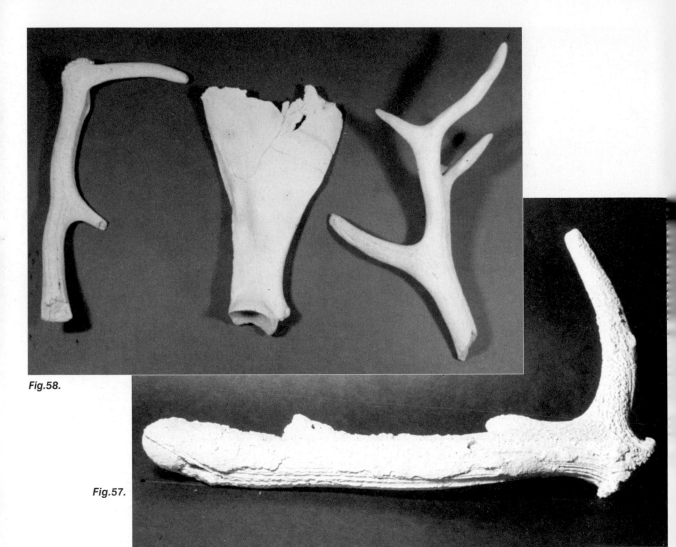

Fig.58.

Fig.57.

Fig.57. The main working tool used by the miners was a red deer antler pick like the example seen in the photograph. All the tines were cut off except the proximal one, and the implement was remarkably efficient, as modern experiments have shown.

Fig.58. The photograph shows a natural antler on the right, and the finished pick on the left. The cow's scapula (shoulder blade) in the centre was used as a shovel.

Fig.59.

Fig.59. This small chalk-cut goddess figurine was reputedly found at Grimes Graves in Norfolk, at the bottom of an unproductive flint shaft, in association with an "altar" of chalk blocks and antler picks. Its provenance is now felt to be dubious.

Fig.60. *The great mound of Duggleby Howe, 9m high, covered a pit filled with skeletons below ground level, together with grave goods. Above the early burials were a series of later cremations, all sealed with a vast capping of clay.*

Thwing (Fig.61.), still 7.5m tall. The former contained a group of collective skeletons, with round bowls (Fig.62.), bone pins and flints, below the old ground surface; despite heavy assaults in the 19th century, the tree-clad Willie Howe still retains its secrets. A similar round mound is Liffs Low near Biggin in Derbyshire, where a skeleton in a stone cist was provided with a superb series of late Neolithic

grave goods (Fig.63.), including pottery, flints, boars' tusks, and other artefacts.

A number of English museums have significant displays of Neolithic material. The Hull and East Riding Museum houses the Mortimer collection from the Yorkshire Wolds, while Sheffield Museum contains the Bateman collection of material from Derbyshire, Stafford and Yorkshire. Devizes, Avebury and Salisbury Museums in Wiltshire likewise have

Fig.61. *Willy Howe, near Thwing, is another monster Neolithic round barrow, though two 19th century openings failed to find any interments. The centre of the site still boasts a huge hollow, the result of the two abortive operations.*

Fig.62. Finely-made round-based bowls of locally produced Grimston ware, and typical of the pottery found with the skeletons under the Duggleby mound.

significant collections from the Wessex locality, including artefacts from the Hoare, Cunnington and Pitt Rivers assemblages, and Dorchester Museum holds other collections from sites in the locality. Other Neolithic material can be seen in the museums in Cirencester and at Woodstock in Oxfordshire. There are also Neolithic displays in the British Museum in London.

Fig.63. A Neolithic skeleton found in a cist at Liffs Low near Biggin was accompanied by a splendid series of artefacts, including a unique pot, a perforated antler mace head, two superb flint axes, boar's tusks, flints and red ochre. These outstanding objects have affinities with those found at Duggleby Howe.

The Bronze Ages

The change from the Neolithic to the Bronze Age in England was a gradual process, and there was a considerable overlap between the two eras. Progress towards metalworking was slow, and occurred at different times in different parts of the country, and the construction of certain monuments cannot be ascribed with certainty to one age or the other.

The Early Bronze Age saw a warmer climate than that of today, resulting in the farming of the higher ground in places such as the northern uplands and Dartmoor. Many small agricultural settlements were established during this time, with pastures and banked-and-ditched enclosures. By the end of the 2nd millennium the climate had become cooler and wetter. Much of the moorlands gradually became encumbered by blanket peat bogs, and the upland settlements were eventually abandoned.

Metalworking became established during the earlier part of the period, and the manufacturing techniques gradually spread over the country. This process had a significant effect on the efficiency of agriculture and crafts. Despite the name given to this era, bronze remained a scarce commodity, and only the rich, with the means to exploit metals such as copper, tin and gold, prospered to any great extent. They may have been the guiding spirits behind the building of specialised barrows, stone circles and monoliths, and a new burial rite under round mounds, with usually single interments accompanied by rare grave goods and pottery.

The population underwent an expansion towards the end of the Early Bronze Age, which may have led to the development of marginal lands and an eventual contest for the more productive soils. This, in its turn, may have created competition and disorder, leading to the construction of defensive sites and refuges, and the development of more efficient weaponry.

Stone circles, avenues and monoliths are intimately linked with henges, and all have firm foundations in the earlier Neolithic, perhaps by the mid-3rd millennium. Most of these monuments occur in the western part of England, where suitable stone was plentiful. The earliest circles were over 30m in diameter, often accompanied by an outlier used to record the rising or setting of the sun or moon, often at midsummer or midwinter.

Good examples of this type of ring are Long Meg and Castlerigg in Cumbria (Fig.64.), the Nine Stones at Harthill in Derbyshire (Fig.65.), and the Rollright Stones in Oxfordshire (Fig. 66.).

Fig.64. Dramatically sited among the Cumbrian hills near Keswick, the Castlerigg stone circle has 38 uprights and is 33m in diameter. A 3m gap on the north side may be an entrance.

Fig.65. A winter view of the Nine Stones at Harthill in Derbyshire. The tallest upright is over 2m high, and several stones have been robbed from the ring in times past. One of them is set in a wall to the south of the monument.

Fig.66. The Rollright Stones in Oxfordshire are part of a fascinating complex, which include the 70-stone King's Men, seen in the photograph, plus the 2.5m high King Stone to the north, and the Whispering Knight's burial chamber further to the east. The monuments are the subject of much folklore, and the King Stone is reputedly the petrified leader of an army represented by the uprights of the ring.

Circles became much larger at the start of the Bronze Age, such as the three at Stanton Drew in Somerset, whose Great Circle had an avenue of standing stones associated with it.

Oval and flattened circles were the next development, together with double and triple rings of stone such as the Hurlers in Cornwall and the Grey Wethers in Devon. Coves - three-sided settings of uprights - can be seen at Avebury (Fig.67.), Stanton Drew, and Arbor Low in Derbyshire, and were the

Fig.67. Coves are three-sided settings of stones found at the centres of a number of prehistoric circles. Two monoliths from one of these features survive at Avebury as part of the northern ring. The distant stone on the left is a survivor of the outer circle.

Fig.68. The Nine Ladies on Stanton Moor is an example of the smaller and later Bronze Age stone circles, which gradually replaced the larger, earlier types.

Fig.69. The Doll Tor circle, also on Stanton Moor, was associated with a burial mound, whose remains can be seen at the bottom of the photograph. There were also burials by cremation at the centre of the ring.

obvious foci for rituals taking place at the sites. Later in the era circles tended to become smaller, perhaps as religion became more locally orientated. Numbers of these more diminutive rings can be seen in Derbyshire (Figs.68&69.), and Yorkshire, many of them embanked. The northern examples are sometimes carved with the so-called cup-and-ring markings

Fig.70. Cup-and-ring marked rocks are largely confined to the northern part of England, and are generally, though not always, connected with the Bronze Age cult of death. Here at Roughting Linn, near Doddington, in Northumberland, a large gritstone boulder is carved with a variety of designs, including groups of cups surrounded by circles and rectangular patterns.

Fig.71. On Gardom's Edge near Baslow, in Derbyshire, is this elaborately incised flat slab close by a settlement of the same date. This rock has now been covered with a permanent copy of the same design.

(Fig.70.), which themselves are often associated with the cult of death. The decorations are pecked and incised (Fig.71.), and sometimes include elaborate concentric circles and spirals, together with abstract patterns such as the very rare swastika (Fig.72.); they are found on rock outcrops, standing stones and burial cists. Good examples occur on Ilkley Moor in West Yorkshire, on the Derbyshire moors, and in Northumberland.

Fig.72. On Ilkley Moor in West Yorkshire is a good, although weathered example of the rare swastika cup-and-ring design. This copy of the original is in Keighley Museum.

Fig.73. *From the centre of Stonehenge the Heel Stone is framed in the uprights of the outer sarsen circle, marking the rise of the sun at midsummer. Note the interlocking lintels, which connect the vertical stones. In the foreground are the smaller and earlier bluestones, whose origins are still a matter of dispute.*

Fig.75. *One of the imposing trilithons forming a horseshoe plan at the centre of Stonehenge. This example is carved with representations of contemporary bronze axes and daggers similar to those found accompanying burials under the surrounding round barrows.*

Fig.74.

Fig.76. The Stonehenge outer circle seen from the eastern side, where it is most perfect. Note that the outer surfaces of the sarsens are far less smoothed than the inner faces of the same stones.

Fig.77. On the eastern side can be seen the so-called "Slaughter Stone", fallen across the edge of the ditch at the entrance to the circle. In reality the stone was one of an upright pair which once stood on either side of the entranceway.

Stonehenge in Wiltshire developed into a sophisticated monument, first with a double ring of bluestones, whose origins remain in dispute, plus the Heel Stone (Fig.73.), marking the rising sun at midsummer, and an earthwork avenue leading to the River Avon. Later, individually shaped sarsens were brought from the Avebury district, and adorned with lintels (Fig.74.), or built up into massive trilithons (Fig.75.), with several apparent celestial and equinoxial targets. This massive circle was remodelled several times during the earlier part of the Bronze Age (Fig.76), and may well have been the great cult centre of the Wessex chiefs (Fig.77.) whose wealth can be appreciated by a study of the grave goods in the surrounding clusters of round barrows grouped across their territories on the surrounding Salisbury Plain.

Fig.74. A view of the most complete part of the outer circle at Stonehenge, with the re-used dolerite bluestones placed in a ring in front of them. All the lintels were shaped to form part of the arc of the circle, and are themselves curved. They were butted to each other and fixed to the uprights by adaptations of woodworking joints.

Fig.78. *In Wessex round barrows are grouped in cemeteries such as this nucleated one at Winterbourne Stoke, west of Stonehenge. The group are partly aligned on an earlier long barrow, seen at the bottom left. Various types of "Wessex" type barrows can be seen, and the designs are explained in the text. Many of the tumuli have been ploughed-out, and only their ditch rings survive.*

Fig.79. *At Priddy in Somerset, a range of round barrows runs along a crest, forming a linear cemetery. Often these mounds are set in such a position as to be easily seen by travellers in the valley bottom below.*

Fig.80. In stony localities bodies or cremations were often placed in cists, or stone boxes such as the one found in the large Gib Hill cairn, near Bakewell, in Derbyshire. Usually these were set deep in the barrow, but in this case the little vault was built into the top of the mound.

The most frequent Bronze Age monuments to be found in England are round barrows, the burial places of the elite members of the local society. In areas such as Wessex, and the Yorkshire Wolds these mounds are built of earth and chalk; in hilly localities such as the Peak District, they are constructed of stones and are called cairns. In other districts they are built up of stacked turves.

In Wessex and Yorkshire they occur in groups or clusters, either nucleated where they are gradually gathered around a "founder's barrow", as at the Winterbourne Stoke group, west of Stonehenge (Fig.78.), or linear, where they follow the line of a ridge or hill, as at Priddy in Somerset. (Fig.79.). Elsewhere they are often found singly or in smaller numbers, often on high ground where they were easily seen. Large numbers have been destroyed by agriculture or for the sake of their stone. In the Trent Valley in Derbyshire, for instance, numbers have been ploughed out and are only visible as crop or soil marks.

While their burials are usually interred singly, a whole new ritual is observable under excavation. In certain areas rich in soil the mounds are surrounded by ditches, which were a ritual feature, intended to indicate that the interior was a sanctified site, often reinforced by the erection of circles of wooden stakes, usually placed inside the ditch, and renewed over time. The idea that the ditch provided the soil to build the subsequent mound is no longer sustainable. In stony localities the ditch was replaced by a stone ring or kerb. Inside this circular feature the dead were buried over a considerable period of time, either in graves dug out of the soil, or in rock graves or cists (boxes built up of stone slabs) (Fig.80.), covered by small mounds of earth or stones.

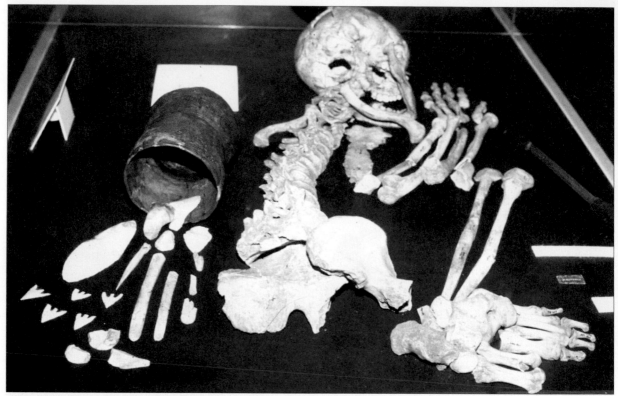

Fig.81. Early Bronze Age burials were crouched in a foetal position, suggesting rebirth. This reconstruction from a Derbyshire cairn shows the beaker and other artefacts placed behind the lower back of the skeleton, though pots and grave goods were sometimes arranged around other parts of the body.

Fig.82. Beakers, the fineware vessels placed with the deceased in the early Bronze Age, are sometimes found in pieces, suggesting they were deliberately broken up. Beaker shards are easy to recognise, both by virtue of their geometrically incised designs, and by the thinness of the fabric. Such fine pots were made only for the dead.

The earliest burial was the *primary*, whilst subsequent ones are known as *satellites*. The dead were crouched up, perhaps in the position suggesting rebirth in a subsequent life (Fig.81.), and were provided with fine pots called beakers, filled with mead to sustain them on their journey to the afterlife (Figs.82-89.). In the Midlands and north other vessels called food vases (Figs.90-91.) were often substituted for the former.

Fig.83. Beaker pots were filled with some kind of mead-like drink, for the refreshment of the spirits of the deceased on their journey to the afterlife. There were a number of different designs, as these Peak District examples show. From left to right they include: long necked, short necked and bell styles. Note the variant patterns, made by grooved and comb tools.

Fig.84. The superb quality of certain beakers can be appreciated in this view of an example from Derbyshire in Sheffield City Museum. Note the carefully executed zoned decoration, and the elegant shape of these hand-made vessels.

Fig.85. Two more graceful vessels, seen here with a stone archer's bracer and flint barbed-and-tanged arrowhead from the same interment. The fragmentary bell-beaker on the bottom right was usurped by the later necked beaker from a site in South Derbyshire.

Fig.86. A splendid grave group from Green Low in the Peak District, where a long-necked beaker burial was accompanied by a quiverful of barbed-and-tanged arrows, a flint dagger and scrapers, bone strips forming a composite bow, and a bone pin. The male found in this grave would be well equipped for hunting in the hereafter.

Fig.87. A display of well-made beakers from the Wessex locality, accompanied by a variety of grave furniture, including, left to right: an archer's wrist guard, a flat bronze dagger, two rare gold basket earrings, three barbed-and-tanged arrowheads, a flint, and an implement made from an animal rib.

Fig.89. A beaker grave group from a barrow at Towthorpe on the Yorkshire Wolds. The burial was equipped with some exceptional artefacts, including a fine flint dagger, a perforated stone battleaxe, and a large jet V-button.

Fig.90. Food vessels seem to represent a merging of Neolithic designs with the new beaker styles. This beautiful vase from Yorkshire exhibits well the main traits in the new patterns, including the deep grooves and intervening lugs. The motifs were again made with comb and grooved impressions. These pots often replaced beakers in later Bronze Age graves. They have never been found together.

Fig.91. A rare handled food vessel from a cairn at Ryestone, near Parwich in Derbyshire. On this unusual vessel the patterns were made by twisted cord impressions. The two flint knives came from a cist grave in the same tumulus.

Fig.92. A good example of the round-headed type of skull exhibited by the early Bronze Age beaker-using immigrants, whose crania were markedly different to those of the Neolithic era. This skull came from a disarticulated individual found in a cist at Bee Low (see Fig.88.).

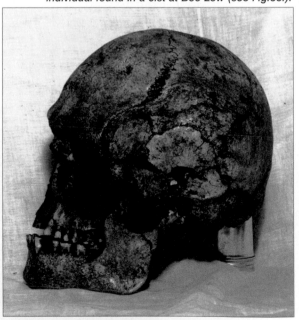

The skulls of these interments are usually *brachy-cephalic* or round-headed, by contrast with Neolithic ones, suggesting another racial group (Fig.92.). Weapons, tools and jewellery were often provided for the dead; these included barbed-and-tanged arrow-heads (Fig.93.), and the remains of bows, flint daggers, stone archer's bracers, and perforated battleaxes (Fig.94.). Bronze artefacts included flat axes (Fig.95-97.), riveted daggers, and awls. Jet and shale in the form of fine necklaces (Figs.98&99.), buttons and rings are fairly common in Derbyshire and Yorkshire, while in the south amber and faience was utilised for the same purpose (Fig.100.). The raising of the covering mound was only the last stage in a whole complex of religious activities, and the barrow sites may have been left open for many years as burials accumulated in the interior of the ditched or kerbed ring.

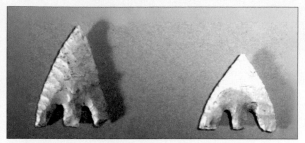

Fig.93. Two finely chipped barbed-and-tanged flint arrowheads found at Green Low (Fig.86.) and missed by the 19th century diggers. This pair was found by the author in the same grave pit, and were reunited with their three companions 118 years after the original opening.

Fig.94. The artisans of the period were responsible for the manufacture of some superb perforated stone battleaxes, usually made for display or gift-exchange by the nobility of this period. Made from a variety of stone, these examples must have been highly prized by their owners.

Fig.95. Bronze axes underwent several design changes during the age, ranging from the early flat axe on the left, made in an open mould, to the palstave in the centre with its stop ridges and hanging loop, and the two-piece socketed example on the right, all three forming a typological sequence.

Fig.94.

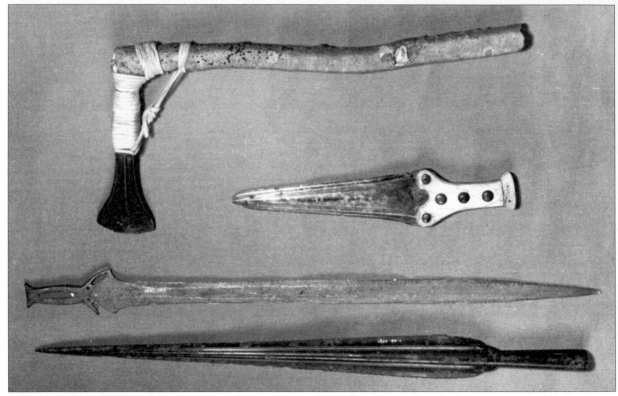

Fig.96. *An assortment of bronzes from the era, including the flat axe at the top, showing the method of hafting. A bronze riveted dagger, with decorated handle and pommel can be seen at the centre, plus a later leaf-shaped sword and socketed spearhead at the bottom of the photograph, the latter showing the increasing predilection for warfare.*

Fig.97. *Further designs in bronze and gold from the Bronze Age, including decorated flat axes, riveted and tanged daggers, and a lunalate and amber button cover made from sheet gold.*

Fig.99. *A beautiful jet barrel bead, accompanied by broken flint leaf and barbed-and-tanged arrowheads, from a Peak District cairn. The deceased had probably not the funds for a full necklace, and had to be satisfied with a single bead.*

52

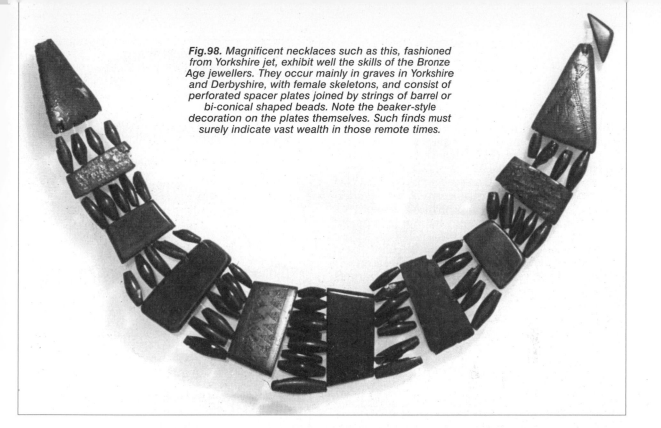

Fig.98. Magnificent necklaces such as this, fashioned from Yorkshire jet, exhibit well the skills of the Bronze Age jewellers. They occur mainly in graves in Yorkshire and Derbyshire, with female skeletons, and consist of perforated spacer plates joined by strings of barrel or bi-conical shaped beads. Note the beaker-style decoration on the plates themselves. Such finds must surely indicate vast wealth in those remote times.

Fig.100. In southern England jet was replaced by either shale or, for the richer element, Scandinavian amber. This Wiltshire female was interred with this exquisite seven-strand necklace made from the latter material, and mixing spacer plates with barrel, bi-conical and ring beads.

In Wessex and other parts of southern England barrows often assumed variant shapes as well as the ubiquitous bowl type (Fig.101.). These "fancy" barrows included bell (Fig.102.), disc (Fig.103.), saucer, and pond varieties. Some seemed to have served particular purposes; bells usually cover male burials, and discs females. Ponds appear to have been constructed for ritual purposes and rarely contain interments.

Sometimes barrows are grouped in pairs ("twin barrows") or more rarely in threes ("triple barrows") (Fig.104.). There is even one example of a quadruple barrow!

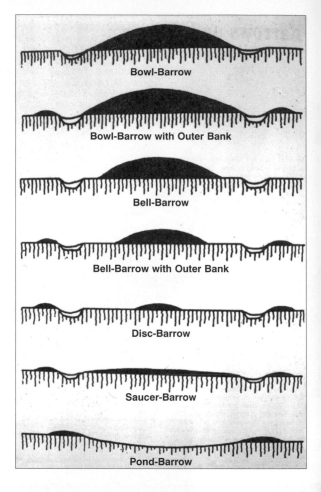

Bowl-Barrow

Bowl-Barrow with Outer Bank

Bell-Barrow

Bell-Barrow with Outer Bank

Disc-Barrow

Saucer-Barrow

Pond-Barrow

Fig.101. In Wessex and other parts of southern England, barrows assumed a variety of shapes, as shown in the illustration. The designs show a descending order of priority, with bowls the most popular, and ponds the scarcest.

Fig.102. A fine example of a bell-barrow, from the Poor Lot cemetery, near Kingston Russell in Dorset. This excellent specimen stands 6m high, and has never been opened. Bells are supposedly the preserve of rich males.

Fig.103. *A disc-barrow in the Oakley Down cemetery in Dorset. They consist of an outer bank, ditch and central "tump" or tumps, which usually cover female cremations. Other barrows can be seen in the background.*

Fig.104. *A triple barrow situated on a ridge above Weymouth. Such close-placed features, often enclosed within a communal ditch, are rare and are felt to cover family burials.*

Fig.105. Small and distinctive pottery vessels such as the slotted cup (left), lidded "Aldbourne" cup (centre), and grape cup (right) are peculiar to Wessex burials and are seldom found elsewhere. Note the pointille decoration on the lid of the Aldbourne example.

Fig.107. Decorated gold breastplate from the Clandon Barrow, perhaps once fitted to a leather back plate and worn on the chest. Note the geometric pattern with similarities to that on the pottery of the time.

In Wessex, several barrows have covered rich burials, with gold, amber, diminutive pottery vessels (Fig.105) and other rare materials. Two of the best examples are the Clandon Barrow on the Dorset Ridgeway (Figs.106&107.), and Bush Barrow, near Stonehenge, felt to be the last resting place of the builder of the last phase of the circle (Fig.108.).

Fig.108. The Bush Barrow, at Normanton just west of Stonehenge, may have covered the builder of the final phases of the great monument. Laid out on his back, the chieftain had a rich array of grave furniture, including the items shown in the plate that include: two bronze daggers, one with a handle set with tiny gold pins, a bronze palstave, and a mace head, made from a fossil pebble, with three unique zigzag bone mounts fixed to the handle.

Fig.106. This shale mace head from the Clandon Barrow in Dorset boasts five circular depressions fitted with bosses of sheet gold. Found with a cremation, it was doubtless a symbol of great authority.

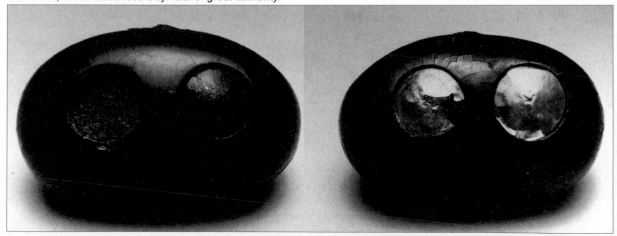

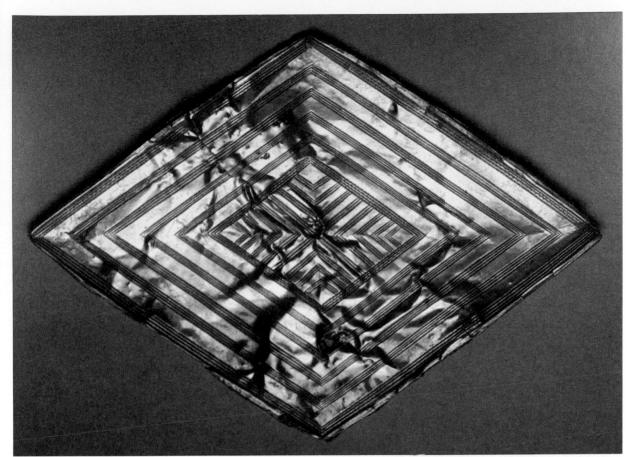

Fig.107.

Fig.108.

Fig.109. *Several Wessex barrows covered burials with gold-work, including the items seen here such as sheet gold, cones and other articles covered with the precious metal. Such burials also sometimes include a series of canister-like gold beads, fashioned so precisely that they almost seem machine-made.*

Fig.110. *Grave group from the vanished barrow at Hove. The artefacts accompanying the burial include an amber cup, a superb stone double-axe, a whetstone pendant with traces of the cloth wrapping still surviving on its surface, and a riveted bronze dagger.*

Fig.111. Barrows often contain an assortment of flint flakes and implements distributed throughout the mound material. Examples include this flint knife with a nicely serrated edge.

Fig.113. Other common flints comprise a selection of scrapers like the "thumb-nail" type on the left, and the discoidal example on the right.

Other rich barrows include the Manton "Gold Barrow" in Wiltshire (Fig.109) and the now-destroyed barrow at Hove in Sussex (Fig.110), both of which covered rich interments. Good examples of barrow cemeteries, apart from those already mentioned, include the Oakley Down group, near Blandford in Dorset, and the Lambourn Seven group in Berkshire. Many others worth seeing exist singly, like Gib Hill, near Arbor Low, or the Deverel barrow near Dorchester.

Later on in the period inhumation burial was gradually replaced by cremation. Indeed both practices seem to have carried on side-by-side for a time, and skeletons are often accompanied by cremations apparently deposited at the same period. Mounds also contain flints, often scattered throughout the barrow material, and perhaps sometimes scraped up when the covering heap was constructed. Examples of these flints can be seen in Figs.111-114.

Fig.114. A random cluster of flints such as this includes scrapers, blades, and the fine petit tranchet arrowhead at bottom left.

Fig.112. Flakes are common finds in barrows, and include knives and blades, such as the plano-convex "slug" knife in the centre of the group.

Fig.115. A small cremation deposit recovered from Bee Low (Fig.88.), and probably once wrapped in cloth. This was found in association was the small riveted dagger seen at the bottom right.

Eventually cremations (Fig.115.) took precedence over un-burnt bodies, the burnt bones being placed in various kinds of urns, or in skin bags. While the so-called collared urn was common throughout England, there were regional variants, which are illustrated in Figs.116-122. Accompanying many cremations were *accessory vessels*, small cups that perhaps served to bring the fire to the cremation pile (Fig.123.). Cremations were often deposited as *secondaries* dug into the covering mounds which overlaid the earlier occupants of the barrow (Fig.124.). Often many millennia after the erection of these tumuli, later races such as the Romans and Anglo-Saxons would place their dead in the upper surfaces of the barrows. These interments are known as *intrusives*. Cairns and barrows became smaller over time, and grave goods eventually disappeared. Good examples of these later cemeteries can be seen on Stanton Moor, and Big Moor, Derbyshire (Fig.125.), and Danby Rigg, North Yorkshire.

Fig.116. Collared urns were the commonest receptacles for burnt bones in the early Bronze Age. These finely made examples from Crookes, near Sheffield, had a burned bronze dagger placed among the deposit, plus a flint leaf arrowhead, and a small accessory vessel pierced by two holes.

Fig.117. A typical collared urn, used both for cremations or domestic storage purposes. Note that all urns were only decorated on their upper parts and almost never below the shoulder.

Fig.118. The potters in different localities produced variations on the collared urn theme. In the south-west urns with horseshoe patterns became common. Note the lower design produced with the aid of a circular piece of stick.

Fig.116.

Fig.118.

Fig.117.

Fig.119. By the end of the early Bronze Age urns in parts of England became cruder, less well-fired, and adorned with rough patterns produced by sticks or fingernails, like these bucket urns from Wessex.

Fig.121. Reminiscent of food vessel designs were these examples with deep collars and narrow pedestal bases.

Fig.120. Another variant form was the barrel or globular urn, with a decoration similar to those found on the earlier beakers.

Fig.122. *Two coarser representations of cinerary urns from Buxton Museum. The heights of such pots varied from around 15cm to 40cm (or even higher).*

Fig.123. *Accessory vessels were usually bi-conical or bowl shaped pots, although occasionally the design resembled miniature examples of the larger collared urn. They could have been used to carry the flame to ignite the funeral pyre, as many have soot-blackened insides, but their purpose is still obscure.*

Fig.124. Model of a Bronze Age round cairn, showing a primary crouched skeleton in a cist, with a secondary urn placed on the capstone of the vault.

Fig.125. The restored drystone bank of a ring-cairn on Big Moor, Derbyshire. Cremations were usually placed inside the circle.

Fig.126. *A hut circle, entrance in the foreground, at the Backstone Beck enclosure on Ilkley Moor. A substantial wall enclosed the farmstead, which had a burial area on the north side. The two adjoining huts may have been for storage, as no traces of occupation were found during their excavation.*

There are few traces of Bronze Age settlements in England, and where found these tend to occur in the stonier areas of the north and west, where their foundations can be seen in parts of Cumbria, Yorkshire and Northumberland. They can also be observed in Devon and Cornwall. On Dartmoor the odd "pound" survives, consisting of a few hut circles, ringed by a substantial stonewall, like Grimspound, a good example of the series.

A similar type of site, although smaller, is Backstone Beck on Ilkley Moor in West Yorkshire (Fig.126.). There are often "reaves", Bronze Age field walls, surrounding the settlements, and showing the presence of an agricultural economy. A few defensive hilltop enclosures began to appear in parts of central and southern England towards the close of the period, including Mam Tor in Derbyshire, and Ram's Hill in Berkshire, while at Flag Fen near Peterborough an artificial island was constructed on waterlogged ground, built of brushwood and timber. The site has some good reconstructions of the timber and thatched round houses of the period. Others existed in parts of East Anglia, Yorkshire, Lincolnshire and Somerset, in the wetter fenland localities. Metalworking skills increased during the period, and by the beginning of the 1st millennium BC, the bronze smiths were turning out a variety of advanced designs and products, such as those shown in Figs.127&128.

A number of museums in England house Bronze Age material. Sheffield Museum has the Bateman Collection, which contains an impressive assemblage of pottery and artefacts, mainly culled from burial mounds in Derbyshire, Stafford and Yorkshire. The Mortimer Collection in Hull has a similar display from barrows on the Yorkshire Wolds. Salisbury, Devizes and Dorchester Museums have the collections of Hoare, Cunnington, Pitt Rivers and other activists busy digging in Wiltshire and Dorset. The Greenwell and other Bronze Age assemblages can be seen in the British Museum, while other more modest selections from the era can be viewed in smaller museums such as Buxton.

Fig.127. Samples of the skills of the bronze smiths can be appreciated in this illustration of later Bronze Age weaponry, which includes grooved, riveted and tanged daggers and two decorative flat axes, perhaps intended as gifts for deities, and thrown into lakes or rivers.

Fig.128. A leaf-shaped sword of the later Bronze Age, together with its decorative chape. Such artefacts strongly suggest warfare in the troubled latter part of this era.

The Iron Age

By the beginning of the Iron Age, circa 800 BC, the English climate was much as it is today. Agriculture was still the staple way of living, with a network of scattered farms and homesteads spread across the landscape, and a series of associated field systems linked by hollow ways, demarcated by ditches and dykes. There was a great demand for iron, after the earliest prospectors and traders had established its value as a metal. By the end of the Bronze Age a series of sizeable hilltop enclosures, protected by banks and ditches, suggest cattle herding, while smaller protected hilltops indicate the start of deliberate fortifications (Fig.129.). These gradually developed into bigger hillforts with extensive bank-and-ditch structures, often consisting of two or more ramparts built of stone, earth or timber, or a combination of these, and acting as the command centres of sizeable territories.

Fig.129. The Uffington Castle hillfort stands close by the famous White Horse (Fig.164.), and commands the Ridgeway prehistoric track running from right to left across the landscape. This small (3h) example boasts an inner bank, deep ditch and counterscarp feature.

Fig.130. *Chieftains in East Yorkshire often defined their extensive territories by building "frontier" demarcation lines such as this series of wide ditch-and-bank earthworks which crossed large parts of the Wolds.*

These areas, such as those on the East Yorkshire Wolds, were sometimes divided by a series of linear dykes or ditches that delineated actual chiefdoms (Fig.130). Few hillforts seem to have been permanently occupied, with most of the population living in small farmsteads or villages, at the centre of their field systems, which were divided by trackways and hedges, lined with drainage ditches. The hillforts in many localities were utilised only for shelter for people and their animals in time of imminent danger either from rustlers, raiders or neighbouring tribes. The Iron Age ended in Southern England with the Roman invasion in AD 43, although it persisted for longer in central and northern areas, until the Roman army penetrated into these territories.

There is a vast difference in the sizes of the so-called hillfort defences in England, ranging from a few hectares to the monster Stanwick site in North Yorkshire, almost 300h in extent. Hillfort defences varied from simple wooden stockade fences (Fig.131.) to double or triple stone-and-timber laced ramparts with deep fronting ditches as at Maiden Castle near Dorchester. The actual centres were carefully chosen to make the best use of the locality in question. *Contour* forts, such as Almondbury near Huddersfield (Fig.132.) and Mam Tor near Castleton

Fig.131. The earliest hillfort defences were simple stockades comprising vertical timbers cross-braced at intervals, as at this reconstruction.

Fig.132. Castle Hill, Almondbury, which is prominently sited on a steep hill overlooking Huddersfield, features contour defences consisting of a double bank and ditch. The ramparts have been partly obliterated by a later Norman motte and bailey castle. The tower in the foreground was erected to celebrate Queen Victoria's Golden Jubilee.

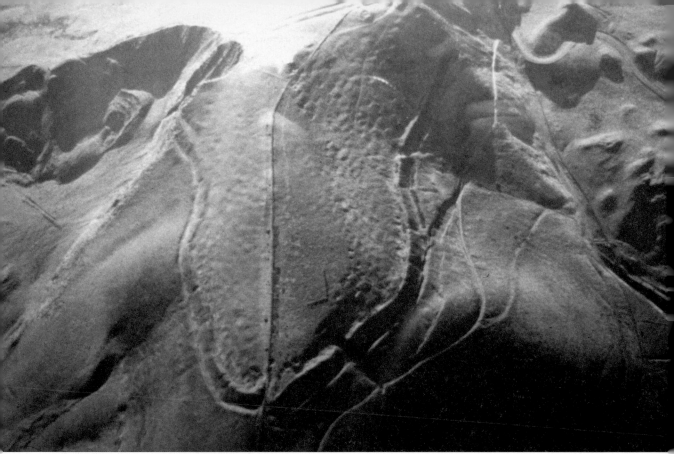

Fig.133. Mam Tor, Castleton, was begun in the late Bronze Age, but the defences were augmented later in the Iron Age. Note the in-turned entrance at the nearer end of the spur. The series of circular depressions inside the banks are the remains of huts, set below the summit presumably to avoid the winds that sweep across the hill.

Fig.134. The oval shaped Warham, Dorset, plateau fort deploys a deep double-bank, with an intermediate ditch, for protection. The entrance can be seen lower right.

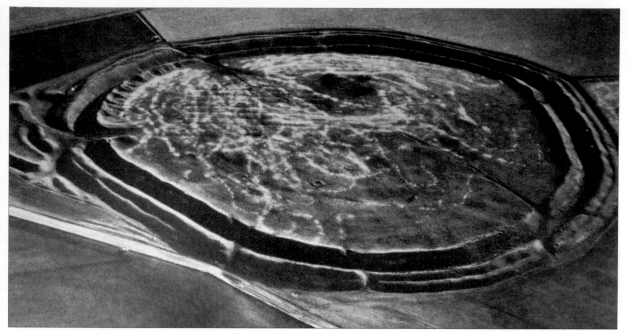

Fig.135. Another plateau fort is this one at Yarnbury. The double bank and ditch are augmented by the well-defended entrance seen on the left. These fortifications include the in-turning of the inner bank, plus a series of outworks giving extra support.

in Derbyshire (Fig.133.) followed the slopes of a hill. *Promontory* forts cut off a steeply sided cliff, spur or promontory, and *plateau* forts, like Warham in Dorset (Fig.134.) and Yarnbury in Wiltshire (Fig.135.) defended an elevated area of lower ground with steep multiple banks and ditches.

Massive hillforts, like Badbury Rings in Dorset (Fig.136.), made use of the whole of a raised area.

Fig.136. Badbury Rings is one of the most massive and spectacular of the southern English hillforts, and has never been excavated. Possibly the result of more than one phase of construction, the defences envelop an entire eminence, forming a meeting point for a junction of later Roman roads.

Fig.137. Hambledon Hill in Dorset occupies a long narrow ridge, and its multivallate defences enclose an area of over 12h. This splendid hillfort has three entrances, and the hollows of numerous hut platforms can be seen, scooped out of the slopes.

Great care and skill was employed to protect the gate or gates, the weakest part of each defended site, and various devices were deployed to give added safety as at Danebury in Wiltshire. Some sites were provided with groups of four or five post structures identified as storehouses or granaries, and most of the larger ones contain round huts which may have been lived in on a permanent basis. Sites such as Danebury also had deep pits for the long-term storage of grain. The bigger hillforts may have functioned as trade centres for the exchange of goods, or as at Hambledon Hill (Fig.137.), the tribal capitals of their chiefdoms.

Over the centuries defences became more elaborate, with the simple wooden fences being replaced with thick drystone-faced walls as at Stanwick (Fig.138.), or box-ramparts filled with soil and stones. Sometimes the box structures were deliber-

ately fired, producing a vitrified wall containing the solidly-fused mixture of stone, timber and earth. Some forts remained uncompleted, and these reveal details of their construction techniques, such as Ladle Hill in Hampshire. By the end of the period, large trading and commercial centres called *oppida* appeared in Southern England, surrounded by massive banks and ditches, and devoted to commerce with the Roman Empire. Such sites include those at Winchester and Colchester.

There is a paucity of burial sites in Iron Age England. In many areas the rite was scattered cremation or interment in flat cemeteries, which leave little or no trace on the landscape. On the East Yorkshire Wolds there were cemeteries of usually small round barrows surrounded by round or square profile ditches (Fig.139.).

Fig.138. At Stanwick in North Yorkshire the fortifications consisted of a rock-cut ditch 5m wide and 12m deep, set in front of a dry-walled stone rampart topped with a wooden palisade.

Fig.139. These square ditches once surrounded small barrows covering the bodies of members of the Parisian tribe of the East Yorkshire Wolds, and arranged in cemeteries sometimes consisting of hundreds of tumuli.

Fig.140. Several dismantled cart or chariot burials have been unearthed under Parisian barrows. This interment, with the iron wheel-tyres and bronze horse equipment, plus the crouched skeleton of their owner, has been reconstructed in the Hull and East Riding Museum.

Fig.141. A fine pair of iron bridle bits, with well-preserved bronze terminals, from a chariot grave on the Wolds.

Three-link bridle-bit with bronze terminals. There is a bronze

Fig.142. A skull from a male Parisian barrow burial. Note the perfectly preserved skull, with its full set of teeth.

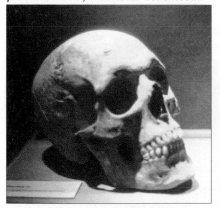

Plough damage has eradicated many of these, though the remnants of some still exist, as at Arras and the Dane's Graves, near Kilham. They contain crouched skeletons, with grave goods including jewellery or martial equipment such as swords. Some of the richer burials are interred with carts or chariots (Figs.140-144.), and belong to the tribe known as the Parisi.

Fig.143. In this grave the two chariot wheels have been stacked at the side of the pit. The horse harness and other artefacts can be seen behind the interment, whilst pork joints have been provided as food for the journey to the afterlife.

Fig.144. Another view of the same grave pit showing the pair of chariot wheels, and the yoke for the horses on top of the cut-away column of soil. Note the fine preservation of the bones of the skeleton. Females as well as males have accompanied chariot burials.

Fig.145. The splendid Battersea bronze shield, found in the River Thames, and obviously placed there as an offering to the gods of the river by a member of the Belgae. The fine curvilinear decoration includes early examples of enamelling.

Fig.146. A distinctive Celtic bronze shield boss found at Wandsworth. The design has similarities to Fig.145., and includes the stylised heads of ducks.

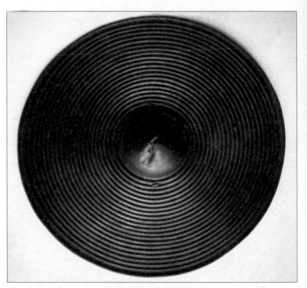

Fig.147. More prosaic is this circular bronze shield from Brigantian territory. Whilst the previous ones are parade items only, this sort of artefact could well have been used in battle.

Fig.148. This iron mirror, presumably mounting a frontal bronze plate, was found with the female skeleton shown in the grave illustrated below the artefact. The somewhat plain handle is set with bronze fittings.

In Southern England other important burials suggest wealthy members of society, men or women accompanied by swords, shields (Figs.145-147.), mirrors (Figs.148-149.) fine "safety-pin" style brooches (Fig.150) and metal boxes (Fig.151.).

Fig.149. Superb bronze mirrors like this example from a grave at Desborough, in Northamptonshire, exemplify the skills of the Iron Age craftsmen. Note again the curved design motifs and the beautifully executed handle. The fronts of such fashion accessories were highly polished to enable their users to see their features clearly.

Fig.148.   Fig.149.

Fig.150. Safety-pin brooches such as these were used to
    fasten cloaks and other apparel, and again display the
curvilinear ornament beloved of the Celts. This distinctive
    specimen has a stylised human face visible at the top.

Fig.151. A cylindrical bronze thread box with incised and
enamelled designs, and fitted with a securing chain for
suspension from a belt. Alongside it is an iron swan's
neck pin with a gold terminal.

Fig.152. *This outstanding bronze Belgic horned helmet also came from the Thames, and was presumably another gift to the river gods. Note the delicate rivet heads holding the piece together, and the characteristic twisted style decoration. The base ring probably held a securing chinstrap.*

Fig.153. *A Belgic grave group from Kent, comprising a cremation with appropriate food and drink placed in plates, cups and flagons. Most of the vessels are imports from the Roman world, showing the extent of trade between the south-east of England and the Empire.*

As well as the remarkable Battersea Shield, found in the River Thames, and illustrated earlier, a superb helmet (Fig.152.) was also found in the river and, like the former, is in the British Museum. Rare objects such as these were for prestige only, for parade and display, and not for use in battle.

In the south-east the Belgic invaders practised cremation in pits, again with grave goods (Fig.153.), while the huge Lexden tumulus near Colchester may have covered the burnt bones of a Trinovantian prince.

In the south-west, inhumation burials were sometimes placed in cists, as at the Harlyn Bay cemetery near Padstow in Cornwall (Fig.154.).

Fig.154. In Cornwall a remarkable Iron Age burial-ground was unearthed at Harlyn Bay in the early 20th century. It consisted of single interments in stone cists, covered for many centuries by sand. Some of the cists were later displayed under glass covers.

Fig.155. This reconstruction of an Iron Age hut was based on an example excavated at Pimperne in Dorset. Large amounts of thatch and clay were needed to complete the rebuilding of this structure.

Fig.156. Although this hut belongs on a Welsh site at Castell Henllys, it is very similar to huts excavated on English sites such at Little Woodbury in Wiltshire. The dwelling in the photograph was erected on the foundations of an original building.

The types of round houses lived in during the Iron Age can perhaps best be appreciated by visiting reconstructed examples such as those at Butser in Hampshire, or Castell Henllys near Cardigan (Figs.155&156.), although remains of homes lived in during the period can be seen on Dartmoor (Fig.157.) and near Harthill in Derbyshire (Fig.158.).

Fig.157. The ruins of stone huts still exist at Grimspound on Dartmoor. The drystone walls and entrance portals can easily be traced on the ground. Another hut can be seen on the left, and in the distance, the perimeter wall surrounding the settlement.

Fig.158. Near Harthill, in Derbyshire, are the ruins of several huts, with paved floors and upright stones forming the walls. Several of these have been excavated and have furnished proof of the period during which they were raised.

Fig.157.

Fig.158.

Fig.159. *For most of the Iron Age pottery was hand-made and consisted mainly of shouldered bowls of various sizes, often decorated with incised motifs like the two on the left. Wooden vessels of different types must have furnished a large part of the culinary ware of the time, although most of this material has not survived.*

Where excavated, these sites provide evidence for the pottery used for much of the period, usually hand-made (Fig.159.), as the potter's wheel only arrived with the Belgae in the last century BC. Weaving combs (Fig.160.) and loom weights show that cloth production was a cottage industry, carried out on the upright looms doubtless used, and for which there is some archaeological proof (Fig.161.).

Fig.160. *These weaving combs and bone skewer pins found on Iron Age sites show that weaving cloth was a cottage industry during the period.*

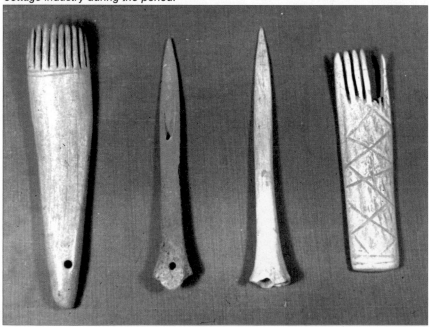

Fig.161. Full scale model of the kind of upright loom in use during the Iron Age. Note the weights holding the warp threads taut; samples of these finds occur on a number of sites. Evidence for this kind of equipment has likewise turned up at settlements such as Staple Howe, near Scampston in East Yorkshire.

Fig.162. Iron Age field systems can be found in many areas that have been untouched by later farming. Here the banks between the fields are clearly visible, and a connecting lane runs left to right just above the centre of the photograph.

Fig.164. This famous white horse at Uffington is probably the tribal emblem of the society who created it. Representations of the animal are found on contemporary coins and other objects. Its survival is remarkable, considering its 2,000 years-plus age.

Fig.163. The Greek gold stater at the top left was the model for many Celtic coins, which were largely copies, produced in various metals including gold, silver, bronze and tin. Note how the original Greek design of a chariot and horses has broken down over time under the Celtic obsession with curving abstract shapes.

In certain areas the field systems around their settlements can still be seen from the air, where subsequent ploughing has not eradicated the banks dividing them (Fig.162.). Coinage was introduced by the Belgae, based on the Greek gold stater, which was extensively copied although the original designs underwent considerable changes (Fig.163.).

Tribal symbols are rare, but the chalk-carved horse near Uffington in Oxfordshire, 110m in length, may well be an emblem or totem of the Iron Age tribe who carved it. (Fig.164.). Other emblems include the so-called "Celtic" stone heads found in northern England, dating from the same era, and which could have been representations of the human heads severed for trophies in a less civilised time (Fig.165.).

Again many English museums contain objects from the Iron Age. The Hull and East Riding Museum has many local artefacts, plus a reconstructed chariot burial from the Wolds. The British Museum houses a number of important objects and reconstructions. Most other regional museums house collections from sites of this period.

Fig.164.

Fig.165. In Northern England stone heads of the period are fairly common finds, like these examples from Keighley Museum. They are felt to be substitutes for the earlier real severed heads collected by less civilised members of the local Iron Age society.

The Roman Period

Fig.166. *This tile from the Legionary bathhouse in York is stamped with the logo of the IX Legion, who were one of the four original legions involved in the invasion of Britain in AD 43.*

Fig.167. *Another of the invading forces was the XX Legion, whose running boar emblem can be seen on this antefix tile once forming part of the roof of a military building.*

Although Julius Caesar paid visits to Southern England in 55 and 54 BC, these adventures did not constitute a conquest, as his "invasions" left no enduring trace and were doubtless soon forgotten. In AD 43 four legions (Figs.166 & 167.) plus auxiliary support landed at Richborough and headed towards the Belgic capital at Colchester, with heavy fighting on the way. Emperor Claudius joined them as Colchester fell, and received the surrender of the south of Britain.

The following year the army advanced to the south-west, north-west and north, where they eventually established a frontier from Exeter to the Humber along which a new road was constructed - the Fosse Way (Fig.168.). There were several battles, and a number of hillforts were stormed in the south-western push, including the vast Maiden Castle, where the earliest British war cemetery was uncovered in the 1930s (Figs.169 & 170.).

South of the so-called Fosse Way frontier the Romans organised a province studded with semi-permanent garrisons, governed initially from Colchester (*Camolodunum*), but subsequently from London (*Londinium*). This was the so-called Lowland Zone, which was the most developed and the richest part of Britain, and the mineral and agricultural resources were speedily amalgamated into the new economic structure. Romano-British farmers paid taxes both in kind, and in the new coinage, supporting an army of occupation some 40,000 strong, and supplying a fast-growing urban population in the new cities and towns. There were severe pressures on the rural communities, the response being the building of villas managed both by prosperous Britons, and occasionally overseas investors. Some half of Roman Britain was united by the new bureaucracy and by a splendid system of roads, rivers and canals.

This rapid "Romanisation" did have its drawbacks, and there was a backlash around AD 60 in East Anglia, seat of the Iceni tribe, when a dispute over the succession brought about a revolt that focussed the long standing grievances of the native Britons. Led by Queen Boudica, the rebels destroyed Colchester, St Albans (*Verulamium*) and London in a few weeks, before her eventual defeat, and the province took years to recover from the blow to its stability. Resistance in Northern Britain was hardening, and a dispute in Brigantia led to Roman annexation of the territory between 71 and 74.

Fig.168. The Fosse Way Roman road ran from Gloucester to Lincoln and formed the frontier of Roman Britain from 47 to the 60s in the 1st century AD. This aerial view shows the relative straightness of the route.

Fig.169. Celtic war cemetery inside the east gate of the Maiden Castle hillfort near Dorchester, after the storming of the stronghold by the II Legion in AD 44. The bodies of the dead defenders were hastily thrust into speedily dug grave pits, with offerings of food and drink. Many bore evidence of sword cuts or spear wounds, and one skeleton had an iron ballista bolt embedded in his spine.

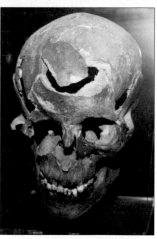

Fig.170. Skull from the ditch of the Stanwick hillfort in North Yorkshire, bearing evidence of a frontal sword cut on the forehead, perhaps inflicted by a legionary during the attack on the fort in AD 71.

Fig.171. A Roman legionary of the 1st century AD, complete with scutum, gladius and pilum.

By the latter date the English portion of Britannia was wholly Roman, and it was only left to complete the conquest of Wales and Scotland.

In the 1st century AD the Roman army consisted of distinct units of *legions* and *auxilia*. The legions (Fig.171.) were the main foundation of the army, and were only Roman in that recruits were citizens of Italian (and later provincial origin), well equipped, trained and disciplined. Their weapons included the *gladius* (short stabbing sword), *pilum* (throwing spear) (Fig.172.), *scutum* (shield), and *pugio* (dagger).

Traces of their metal equipment have been found on many Roman military sites (Figs.173&174.). A full-strength legion contained some 5,200 soldiers arranged in 10 cohorts, themselves further divided into six centuries of 80 men, each century being commanded by a centurion. The first cohort was the biggest, and contained five double centuries. In battle the legions took on the heaviest of the fighting, and in peacetime they carried out all types of civil and military engineering. Legionaries normally served for 25 years, with good, regular pay and a

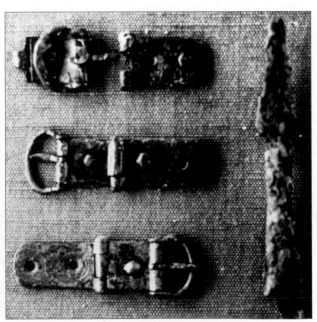

Fig.172. Military artefacts from the Roman period, including bronze belt buckles and fittings on the left, and the head of a pilum on the right.

posts, and kept unofficial wives and families in the adjoining settlements where they often lived out their lives after discharge. Sons followed their fathers into the army, and by the end of the era the force was mainly a Celtic one and largely British.

By 410 the links with Rome were virtually severed, and the soldiers became more or less a native army defending their own homeland. The organisation of the force had altered dramatically with the changes wrought by Emperors Diocletian and Constantine. There was no longer any distinction between legionary and auxiliary, but there was a distinction between the static frontier forces (*limitanei*) and the mobile field armies, known as the *comitatenses*. The former were the less-regarded organisation, retaining what was left of the old legionary structure. The *comitatenses* by way of contrast dealt with enemies who had overran the frontiers, and, in a novel practice, this rapid reaction force were billeted in the fortified settlements. We know relatively little of their living arrangements, but glimpses can be seen in excavations at Portchester in Hampshire, and in barracks at Housesteads on Hadrian's Wall.

The Roman fleet was an adjunct of the army, and had a vital role in liaison and transport, both at the time of the conquest and in later campaigns. Until the 2nd century the force was called the *Classis Britannica*, but it underwent many changes before it patrolled the English Channel under the command of Carausius, or swept the Yorkshire coast and Bristol Channel to intercept raiding forces and to forewarn signal stations positioned there as an early warning system against Saxon incursions.

Among the permanent bases used by the army were the legionary fortresses, massive structures defended by high walls with strong towers and stone buildings inside. Some 20h in extent, they are the larger sisters of the forts which housed the auxiliary contingents. The latter, like the earlier phases of the former, were originally built with turf and timber ramparts, gates with towers, walls with rounded corners, and a series of external V-shaped ditches. They ranged in size from one to three hectares, and were

Fig.174. A magnificent bronze parade helmet with hinged face plate, as worn by an officer in a cavalry unit. This specimen came from the fort at Ribchester in Lancashire.

bonus on discharge as a veteran. The auxiliaries were native soldiers recruited from every part of the Roman world, usually bringing special skills such as archery, slinging, horse riding and tracking. They were similarly organised to the legions, and carried like equipment, but the foot soldiers were only formed to cohort level, and they kept much of their native traditions and personality. Before Roman citizenship was made universal they were guaranteed this boon on discharge, after 25 years' service.

Many Britons served in the army as auxiliaries; they were sometimes posted abroad, and in the fullness of time, when regulations were relaxed, could become legionaries. Both legionaries and auxiliaries spent much of their service in garrison forts and out-

Fig.175. A reconstruction of one of the gates at the auxiliary fort at the Lunt, Baginton, built around AD 60, at the time of the Boudican insurrection. The wooden structures were prefabricated, and could be speedily bolted and fastened together.

Fig.176. A close-up of the gate at the Lunt, showing the openwork nature of the tower, similar to examples shown on military columns such as that of Trajan in Rome.

Fig.177. The unexcavated site of an auxiliary fort can be seen lower right. Note the playing card platform, and the gates visible on the four sides. A double ditch surrounds the fortification, and traces of the internal roads are discernable on the ground.

Fig.178. At the auxiliary fort of South Shields (Arbeia), a stone gateway has been reconstructed on the foundations of the original one. This view shows the front elevation of the imposing structure, with the crenellated flanking walls showing on either side.

sometimes larger. There is a reconstructed example at the Lunt, Baginton, Warwickshire (Figs.175&176.).

Some of these more permanent forts were later rebuilt in stone, this including both the ramparts and internal buildings. The playing card planform (Fig.177.), with four gates (Fig.178.) and two intersecting roads, can be seen at a number of excavated sites (Figs.179&180.). Intramural structures include barrack blocks, granaries, workshops, stables, and a hospital. At the fort centre stood the headquarters building (*principia*) with its courtyard, strong room, shrine for the standards, and an imposing cross-hall. The *praetorium* or commandant's house stood next to the latter, while the bathhouse was always beyond the walls as an anti-fire precaution. Also beyond the walls were the temple and buildings forming the *vicus* or village that invariably grew up outside one of the fort gates to provide off-duty recreation for the garrison.

The marching camp had the same basic layout as the fort. On campaign it was normal for the legion to set up camp every night. This camp consisted of an earth rampart topped with a fence of stakes carried by the troops on the march for this purpose. Wherever possible, this camp was surrounded by a ditch. The leather tents held six men, with bigger individual examples for the officers. The four vulnerable

Fig.179. *Model of the auxiliary fort and associated vicus at Slack near Huddersfield in Yorkshire, and displayed at the Tolson Memorial Museum there. Note the layout of the former, with the main buildings in a line, and the bathhouse at centre left. The vicus, which has its own bank and ditch, boasts a mansio or hostel, which can be seen at the top centre.*

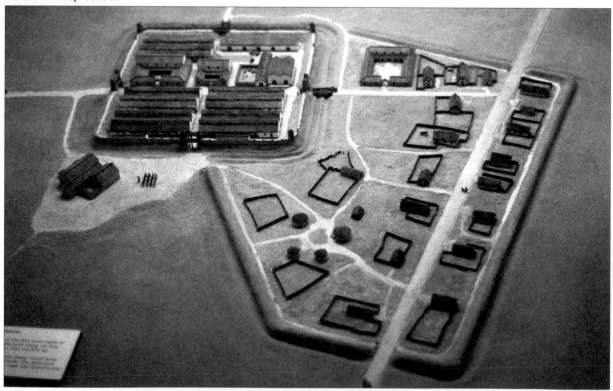

Fig.180. A similar site at Ilkley, where the fort guards the crossing of the River Wharfe, and the vicus clusters near the crossroads to the south. In contrast to Slack, which enjoyed only a short life, this fort remained in existence for most of the Roman occupation.

entrances were protected either by a *clavicula*, a curved continuation of the defensive bank inside the camp, or by a *titulum*, a short rampart and ditch across the external gap in the bank. Temporary practice camps are also found, and are often indistinguishable from the semi-permanent sites; examples can be seen at Cawthorne in North Yorkshire, and Haltwhistle Burn in Northumberland.

The smallest category of permanent sites is the fortlet, a square structure with banks, ditches and stone walls. The milecastles on Hadrian's Wall are a specialised type of this structure, as are the signal stations raised on the Yorkshire coast in the later 4th century. A good example of the latter type is the one at Scarborough in North Yorkshire. Note too, the Hadrian's Wall interval turrets, similar to the watch-towers on the Rhine frontier.

Scotland was never fully Romanised, and the north of Britain was eventually abandoned by Emperor Hadrian, who secured the frontier by the great wall, begun in 122 and completed after many modifications. For many years Hadrian's Wall effectively "separated the Romans from the barbarians" and it continued to serve after the abortive advance into Lowland Scotland in 139, and the adoption of the Antonine Wall as the new, more northerly, frontier.

Fig.181. The now partly silted ditch in front of Hadrian's Wall can be clearly seen on the left of the plate, with the Wall on the right. This stretch of ditch is near the fort at Chesters.

Fig.182. Cleared out section of the flat-bottomed vallum south of the Wall, seen here at Benwell, near Newcastle-on-Tyne. The view shows a regulated crossing, with the remains of a gate, leading to a fort whose south wall once stood on the line of the hedge.

Scotland was finally abandoned in 163, and Hadrian's Wall was re-commissioned. Built between 122 and 127, the latter stretched 117km across the north of England, from the River Tyne to Solway Firth. North of the Wall is a V-shaped ditch

Fig.183. Milecastle 42 still stands west of Housesteads fort at Cawfields, though in a ruinous state. The Wall can be seen curving around the line of the fortlet, which has been cut into the steep hillside. Note the massive stones used in the building of the gateway.

(Fig.181.), and south of it a flat-bottomed ditch traditionally known as the *Vallum* (Fig.182.). At every Roman mile along the structure was a milecastle (Fig.183.), and between each pair of milecastles were two turrets (Figs.184-186.). There were also 16 forts

Fig.184. Brunton Turret 28B, with its associated stretch of Wall, can be seen east of the fort at Chesters. It is in a fine state of preservation.

Fig.185. Turret 52A at Banks East was originally a Turf Wall structure, but was later rebuilt in stone. It stands 11 courses high, and is set in a surviving length of Wall.

Fig.186. At Chesterholm (Vindolanda), the life-size replica of a stone turret has been constructed, together with a few metres of Wall, giving the visitor a good idea of the dimensions of this type of military building.

Fig.187. The first length of Hadrian's Wall still surviving on the eastern part of the line. This short piece, just west of Newcastle-on-Tyne, is 2.9m thick on a 3.2m foundation, and is around 100m long.

on or near the Wall, added at a late date in the construction, and outpost forts to the north.

As first conceived the eastern part of the Wall, from Newcastle to the River Irthing, was built of stone. The western stretch, to Bowness, was constructed of turf. The stone wall was intended to be 3m wide, but much of it is only 2.4m on a 3m foundation (Fig.187.). The original turf wall was later replaced by a 2.7m wide stone wall, completed by 163. The Wall stood perhaps 6m high, with a 1.8m parapet.

The ditch averaged 8.2m across, and 2.7m in depth, while the *Vallum* ditch was 6m wide and 3m deep, its flat bottom about 2.4m wide. The material excavated from this ditch was piled into two continuous banks 9m back from either side of the ditch. This bank and ditch system could only be crossed by causeways at certain selected points, and formed in effect the rearward part of the frontier line of the civilian zone of Roman Britain.

The milecastles provided accommodation for the auxiliary troops patrolling the Wall. They were constructed first, and the Wall was then built up to them. They were all based on a uniform plan, but with slight internal differences. They held up to 50 men, usually in two barracks raised on either side of the road running through the centre of the site. From the beginning of the 3rd century the large milecastle gates providing access to the north, and enabling garrisons to launch attacks on enemy raiders, were part-blocked to postern size, suggesting a cut in the numbers of men available to defend the system. The original turf-wall milecastles were of a similar pattern to the stone ones, but were of turf and timber.

The pair of turrets between each milecastle covered an area of 1.9 square metres. They had two storeys, the upper one probably accessed by a retractable ladder. Some 2,000 men were needed to patrol the Wall and its buildings, and most of these were quartered in the milecastles. To give added support to the garrison, 16 forts were built along the Wall line, each holding 500 to 1,000 men. There were also three outpost forts ahead of the Wall, and a system of forts, fortlets and watchtowers extended the defences for a further 65km along the Cumbrian coast.

Fig.188. *This superb little temple devoted to the god Mithras is outside the unexcavated fort at Carrawburgh (Brocolitia) and was discovered in 1949 during a severe drought. The altars seen here are replicas, and a full-size reconstruction of the site, albeit foreshortened, can be seen in the Museum of Antiquities, at Newcastle University.*

Fig.189. *Part of a barrack block excavated at the Chesters (Cilurnum) fort. The auxiliary troopers were accommodated here in cramped rooms holding up to eight men.*

Fig.190. This elaborate little bathhouse can still be seen at Chesters, alongside the River Tyne. Its survival is due to slopewash that once completely covered the remains, which stand up to 15 courses high at the rear. The usual range of hot and cold rooms is still visible, and the seven alcoves shown in the photograph have been interpreted as lockers, once hung with doors.

A number of the Wall forts have been excavated and are open for inspection. Although varying in size they are more or less uniform in layout. Each presumably had its large extramural *vicus*, for here were born and brought up the succeeding generations of garrison troops; the Wall was manned by Britons and not Romans. Outside the fort walls were the bathhouses for the soldiers, and small temples such as the ones at Carrawburgh and Benwell, to gods such as Mithras (Fig.188.) and Antenociticus.

The forts were standard types, similar to those found in the rest of Britain. They were built with barracks (Fig.189) and stables, and all had bathhouses like the finely preserved example at Chesters (Fig.190.). Granaries provided the staple diet of corn, such as the example at Housesteads (Fig.191.), while the main food stocks for the Wall were kept stored in huge granaries such as the ones at the main supply base at Corbridge (*Corstopitum*), near Hexham (Fig.192.). At two points along the Wall, wooden bridges spanned the River Tyne, at Chesters (Fig.193.) and Willowford (Fig.194.). At both places the remains of the stone abutments for the structures can still be seen.

Hadrian's Wall lost its strategic importance when the Antonine Wall, further to the north, supplanted it but by 163 the latter had been abandoned and the frontier was again established on the Tyne-Solway line. In 196-7 the Wall was badly damaged during incursions by the Picts, and was substantially repaired under Emperor Severus who came to Britain to oversee operations against Caledonia.

A long period of peace followed, broken in 296 when the usurper Allectus withdrew the Wall garrison in an effort to claim the imperial throne. Once more the northern invaders caused serious damage to the Wall, which was made good by 306. The last great barbarian incursion occurred in 369 when a combined force of Picts, Scots (from Ireland), and Saxons overwhelmed the Wall defences and drove south, burning and pillaging as they went. In 369 the Wall was again stripped of its troops for another attempt at seizing the Empire. The soldiers never returned, and Hadrian's Wall was eventually left to the control of native troops and was virtually abandoned as a defence line.

The Wall is the greatest Roman military work, which still survives partly intact. Fortunately, large stretches have been preserved and are open to view. Only by a visit can one really appreciate its rugged grandeur as it rises and falls impressively over the highest points of the northern English landscape.

With a few rare exceptions there are no rural settlements of a distinctively Roman type in England,

Fig.191. The staple diet of the Wall garrison was corn, stored in granaries like the one seen here at Housesteads (Vercovicium). The granary floor was raised on the pillars seen in the photograph, which ensured a flow of air, and kept it hopefully clear of rodents.

Fig.192. Corbridge (Corstopitum), near Hexham, was the major supply base for the Wall, with river access via the River Tyne. The photograph shows one of the huge granaries at the base, robbed down to ground level for the building stones. The footings for the supporting buttresses can be seen around the walls, whilst the stone flooring of the building still survives.

Fig.193. At two points along its route Hadrian's Wall crosses rivers. Here at Chesters can be seen the massive stone abutment on the south side of the River Tyne, which provided a foundation for the structure. The line of the Wall is visible on the right.

Fig.194. At Willowford the Wall crossed the River Irthing via another bridge. A good 800m stretch of the Wall can be seen on the left, and on the right are the footings for the massive abutment for the three piers carrying the structure. The streambed seen here was paved to form an emplacement for a mill wheel.

as the landscape, especially in the Highland Zone, remained relatively uninfluenced by the Romans and life continued much as it had in the late Iron Age period. However, there were other material changes, including the adoption of Roman-style pottery and coinage, and even painted wall plaster. Also, sometimes the circular types of houses were replaced by those in rectangular style, with thatched or tiled roofs, and stone walls. Settlements in Northern England and Cornwall remained very much Celtic throughout the period.

The appearance of auxiliary forts and roads, however, influenced the siting of the new *vici*, which grew up outside the fort gates. Some developed into small market towns at crossroads, and remained on fort sites when the latter disappeared, as at Melandra Castle (*Ardotalia*), near Glossop. Rural industries also played their role as at Charterhouse-on-Mendip, in Somerset. In many cases, too, the landscape configuration has survived, and the so-called "Celtic" fields and terraced strip-lynchets can still be seen. These are often visible in low light, when the shadows pick out the relief, or in autumn and winter when the vegetation is low.

Among the most numerous surviving remains of the Roman era are the road systems, most of which can be easily traced using Ordnance Survey maps at the 1:50,000 scale. Their usual uncanny straightness was often modified to suit the terrain, and their construction varied considerably. The usual configuration was a 3.7 to 4.5m wide section composed of rammed gravel or local equivalent, such as iron slag, laid on a coarser foundation, and often renewed from time to time. Side ditches are invariably present,

Fig.195. An artist's impression of the winged corridor villa at Chedworth in Gloucestershire, embodying a bathhouse on the right, plus formal gardens and a shrine to the genius loci that can be seen near the top centre. The wealth of such villas lay in the fertile fields surrounding the building, and which produced corn on a large scale.

ROMAN REMAINS
MORTON near BRADING
ISLE OF WIGHT. 1880.

Fig.196. An 1880 print of part of the magnificent Brading villa on the Isle of Wight. Note the main suites of rooms with a fine series of mosaic floors. Just above the visitors, shown on the left, can be seen a corridor provided with a tessellated floor.

often at some distance, for drainage and to indicate a zone to be kept clear of vegetation to obviate potential dangers. Travellers using the road system were exempt from the law, which forbade the carrying of weapons in public. The most prominent feature of a Roman road is the *agger* or embankment, present even when it seems structurally irrelevant, and presumably built to impress the traveller. Bridges were usually constructed of wood, whilst milestones are rare. Hot baths and changes of horses were often available at road stations called *mansiones*, provided especially for persons travelling on official business or carrying the state post.

Villas formed part of the complex of the Roman agricultural economy. Strictly speaking a farmhouse or cottage could constitute a villa, but the term should properly include the surrounding land as well. Frequently these small units were later embodied in much bigger and more complex houses. The development of villas is by no means standard, and there are a number of variant plans. Most villas were of the *corridor* type, with the corridor or veranda connecting a series of rooms (Fig.195.). The winged corridor type was often a modification of this, with the wings either extending forwards or forming an "H" plan. The most refined plan was the *courtyard* villa in which suites of rooms or individual buildings were clustered around one or more courtyards. Occasionally they enclosed a walled farmyard or a garden.

Many of the outbuildings were large aisled barns, altered over time by long usage. Corn driers and wells were both introduced by the Romans, the former similar to a small hypocaust.

Within the villa the main room, usually centrally placed, was the dining or reception room, invariably provided with a mosaic floor and painted walls (Fig.196.). Dining rooms were often semicircular in plan, imitating the classical three-couch setting. Other rooms such as bedrooms are difficult to identify, although narrow areas on the plans are thought to represent staircases to upper levels. Kitchens seem rather primitive to modern visitors, whilst bath blocks were often smaller versions of the bigger town suites, usually housed in separate buildings for safety reasons, in the event of fire. The hypocausts for under-floor heating are usually easy to see (Figs.197.&198.), with stone, brick or tile pillars supporting thick floors of concrete, often with mosaic or tessellated upper surfaces. They were warmed by furnaces, which circulated hot air under the hollow floors, then up the walls via hollow box flue tiles. The heated air and smoke was finally expelled through vents under the roof eaves. Hypocausts differ from the heating vents placed underneath living room floors, where the thick masonry between the channels acted as storage heaters for extended and gentle heating. The pillared type could be warmed speedily, as necessary.

Fig.197. Rooms in villa bathhouses were furnished with mosaic floors and underfloor hypocausts for the necessary heating. Here at Chedworth a convenient hole in the floor reveals the pilae or stone and tile pillars supporting the floor itself.

Fig.198. Hypocaust floors were braced by either stacks of tiles, or altar-shaped blocks of stone, as shown in this photograph of rows of pilae under a ruined room at Chedworth.

Fig.199. View of the eastern suite of rooms at Chedworth showing the surviving heights of the robbed-out walls when the villa was discovered in the 19th century.

Good examples of villas worth seeing, with good mosaics, include Chedworth in Gloucester (Fig.199.), Bignor in Sussex, Brading on the Isle of Wight, and Lullingstone in Kent (Figs.200-201.). Perhaps the most splendid mosaic now on view in England is the reconstructed Orpheus example at Littlecote House in east Wiltshire, now a private hotel (Fig.202.). Only a few extra-large villas or palaces have been identified in England, the most famous being at Fishbourne, near Chichester, where the excavated site and its features can be seen and appreciated (Figs.203&204.).

Fig.200. The Lullingstone villa in Kent contains some first-class mosaic floors, including this fine example of a "seasons" mosaic, with representations of spring, summer, autumn and winter in the four corners. In the centre Bellerophon, mounted on the winged horse Pegasus, is shown spearing the Chimera. A group of dolphins can be seen swimming around the main subject of this superb example of mosaic art.

Fig.201. *Another fine Lullingstone mosaic shows the goddess Europa being abducted by Zeus in the shape of a bull, while a despairing cupid vainly pulls at the animal's tail. Note the swastikas in the frieze above, symbols of good luck. Scenes from Classical mythology were very popular with villa owners, who had them commissioned from the local school of mosaicists.*

Fig.202. *The exquisitely restored Orpheus mosaic at Littlecote in Wiltshire. The building is either an Orphic cult centre, or a summer dining room attached to a villa. Orpheus can be seen at the centre of the circle, with a leaping dog, while goddesses ride animals in the quarterings of the circle, each perhaps representing one of the seasons.*

Fig.203. Model of the palace at Fishbourne near Chichester, perhaps originally built for the client king Cogidubnus in the 1st century. Note the bathhouse lower left, and the creek allowing small vessels to anchor alongside the complex.

Fig.204. The Boy-on-a-Dolphin mosaic at Fishbourne, showing a cupld riding the mammal, surrounded by fabulous sea horses, sea panthers and elegant vases.

Fig.205. The centre-piece of a crudely-executed mosaic from the Rudston Villa in North Yorkshire, showing an unlikely Venus holding an apple and dropping a mirror (perhaps after seeing herself!), with a triton bearing a torch in dangerously close attendance.

Fig.206. Another substandard effort from Aldborough Roman town, portraying the Romulus and Remus legend, with a comical-looking she-wolf attempting (without teats) to suckle the unfortunate babies.

Fig.207. The remains of the large and magnificent Woodchester Orpheus mosaic, perhaps laid in the reception room of a provincial governor's palace. Note the circular frieze of beasts circling the destroyed Orpheus centrepiece. Drawings made of this outstanding mosaic, sketched at the time of its discovery, have enabled an exact replica to be constructed near the original site.

Many mosaic pavements survive in the Lowland Zone of Roman Britain. They range from the crude efforts by inferior craftsmen (Figs.205&206.), from sites such as Aldborough and Rudston in Yorkshire, to splendid representations like the one at Woodchester in Gloucestershire (Figs.207&208.), and from plain geometric forms (Fig.209.) to elaborate subject matter and designs (Figs.210-212.). Painted wall plaster has been recovered from a number of buildings in various parts of England. Good examples have been rescued from the villa at Rudston, and can be seen in the Hull and East Riding Museum (Fig.213.).

Fig.208. A detail of one of the prowling beasts, in this case a splendid lion exhibiting a shaggy mane.

Fig.209. A plain but well-executed geometric mosaic from a town house at Aldborough, and still visible on site. Note the typical twisted cabling surrounding the piece, and the stylised swastikas in the black-and-white frame.

Fig.210. *Figures depicted frontally are rare in English mosaics, which makes this victorious charioteer from Rudston Villa in North Yorkshire all the more interesting. The driver, from the red team, checks his four-in-hand whilst holding aloft the trophies of his team's success.*

Fig.211. *Now in the British Museum, the extensive Hinton St Mary mosaic includes the central figure of the Emperor Constantine, framed by the Chi Rho Christian symbol, with representations of probable disciples in each of the four corners.*

Fig.212. *The villa at Brantingham, near Brough in East Yorkshire includes this unusual robed and haloed male figure, which forms part of a mosaic floor.*
The dark red tesserae forming part of the design are in themselves uncommon.

Fig.213. *Good examples of painted wall plaster can be seen at various sites and museums in England. These samples, from the Rudston Villa, can be seen in the Hull and East Riding Museum.*

Fig.214. Many towns erected fortifications at some stage during their existence. A fine length of unexposed walling can be seen in the grounds of Aldborough Manor, at the site of the Roman town of Isurium. Note the column bases rescued from the nearby fields.

Fig.215. An exposed section of the 3m thick sandstone wall at Aldborough. The plinth still survives, and part of an internal tower can be seen on the left. On the right the existing wall is covered by turf.

The tribal administrative pattern existing in pre-Roman Britain was adopted by the Romans for their administrative regions, or *civitates*. Their *civitas capitals* were new Roman towns built either on the sites of Iron Age settlements or on new localities where the power base had to be transferred from a nearby hillfort. The Iron Age aristocracy, who must have owned the new villa estates surrounding the towns, supplied the town magistrates and town council, who were chosen by election. To a great extent the society was self-governing.

The *municipium* was of a more elevated status, with a constitution provided by charter, and whose citizens enjoyed a restricted form of Roman citizenship. There were some half-dozen examples of this kind of establishment in Roman Britain, but the only certain case is St Albans. Four cities enjoyed the highest status of *colonia*, and three of these - Lincoln (*Lindum*), Colchester, and Gloucester (*Glevum*) - were founded early in the conquest, as settlements for retired army veterans, a safeguard against uprisings, and a leading force in the Romanisation process. The other city, York, gained its charter late in the history of Roman Britain, in the early 3rd century; another probable *colonia* may have been London. A *colonia's* constitution was based on that of Rome, and its residents were granted Roman citizenship, although in fact all provincials were given this status by a decree of the Emperor Caracalla in 212.

The larger Romano-British settlements were allowed to build defences, perhaps as a sop to civic pride, rather than any military requirement at this time. Most of these fortifications date from the end of the 2nd century, and consist of easily-erected earthworks, although some towns added stone walls during the following two centuries (Figs.214&215.).

Fig.216. The "Painted House" at Dover has decorated walls still standing some 2m high. Note the hypocaust visible in the floor, and the painted broom leaning against the wall, above the dado.

By the later 4th century, in more dangerous times, there was a need to add artillery bastions and deeper ditches for extra protection. Gateways were always well-provided for, with massive towers and strong wooden gates.

There are often traces of town houses in Roman Britain, in *insulae*, stretches of shops, or in blocks, as at St Albans. At Dorchester (*Durnoveria*) small villas existed in their own grounds. These residences often boasted hypocausts, mosaics and painted plaster, like the villas. A fine example is the so-called Painted House at Dover (*Dubris*), built outside the walls of the earlier fort (Fig.216.). In this regard the latter is similar to the open settlements or *vici*, which grew up outside the auxiliary forts such as Vindolanda and Housesteads on Hadrian's Wall. These residences lack bath blocks, as the local public baths were available for use by the population (Fig.217.).

Fig.217. Public baths like this one at Well in North Yorkshire were intended for the use of the local population. The photograph shows a well-preserved plunge-bath at the site.

Fig.218. Wroxeter (Viroconium) had the most extensive public baths so far uncovered in Roman Britain. This general view across the complex includes the largest section of masonry wall to be found on a civilian site in the province.

Fig.219. A close-up of the masonry wall at Wroxeter, which includes the main entrance to the facility. Note the red tile bonding courses set at intervals in the structure.

Fig.220. The Jewry Wall at Leicester still stands over 7m high, and forms part of the palaestra of the large public baths built in the civitas capital.

These public baths can be best appreciated at places such as Wroxeter (*Viroconium*) (Figs.218&219.) in Shropshire, and at Leicester (*Ratae*) (Fig.220.), where private benefactors or the city authorities provided these sumptuous amenities. Clients undressed in the *apodyterium*, progressed through the *frigidarium* into the warmer *tepidarium*, and then went on to the hot *caldarium* (sited next to the furnace and provided with a hot bath). The steam opened up the pores of the skin, producing sweat, and the dirt was removed by oil and a curved *strigil* or scraping implement. Massage may have been part of the service, followed by a steady progression in reverse back through the rooms to the *frigidarium*, where a cold plunge bath awaited the customer, together with a brisk rubdown with a towel. Plunge baths were intended for immersion only, and the adjoining *palaestra* was an area for physical jerks. At the huge complex at Bath (*Aqua Sulis*) (Fig.221-223.), dedicated to the deities Sulis-Minerva (Fig.224.), the bathhouse at Chesters (Cilurnum), and at other sites, can be seen the *laconicum*, a type of sauna, which involved sweating in dry heat.

Fig.221. Bath (Aquae Sulis) contained hot springs, which attracted Roman settlement. The town developed as a spa dedicated to the deities Sulis-Minerva. The so-called Great Bath can be seen here, with the original Roman work standing as high as the cut-off pillars. Other parts of the complex have been exposed behind the blocked-off arches in the distance.

Fig.223.

Fig.224.

Fig.222. The Sacred Spring at Bath, from which the waters issue at 46.5 C. The masonry is the original Roman stonework.

Fig.223. The water was fed into the baths complex via this culvert, through a system of lead pipes.

Fig.224. The splendid Gorgon's head at Bath, rescued from the fallen pediment of the great temple, and exemplifying the art of the native inhabitants of Britain.

A popular amusement was the entertainment provided by the *ampitheatre*, a structure elliptical in plan form, unlike the semicircular *theatre*. The former (Figs.225&226.), sited outside the walls of a town or city for obvious reasons, was the place for animal sports, gladiatoral combats and the like, with martial shows in garrison towns. Theatres were less common, and were presumably utilised for more dignified recreations (some perhaps of a religious bent) and public meetings.

Fig.225. *A Roman amphitheatre was sited outside the gates of a town, and was the venue for gladiatorial fights and animal sports. Spectators occupied stone or wooden seats, which were separated by a series of entrances as seen in this aerial view.*

Fig.226. *Viewed from one of the entrances, this photograph shows the tiered blocks of seating common to all excavated examples.*

Fig.227. *This colonnade once fronted the forum at Wroxeter, which was on the left of the photograph. The forum and basilica were burned down in the 2nd century, but were subsequently rebuilt on an even more lavish scale.*

The *forum* (Fig.227.) was the market place and municipal area, centrally sited at the junction of the main streets of the grid. On one side was the *basilica*, a large roofed town hall, used to superintend justice and general administration. Official hospitality was dispensed in the *mansio*, a civic inn, or a road station like that at Wall (*Letocetum*) in Staffordshire.

Other public edifices included temples, public fountains and monumental arches. The last two are not well represented in Roman Britain, although there is evidence for the provision of water and the disposal of sewerage. Water was dispensed via aqueducts, usually open streams or channels. The Dorchester example can still be seen, and part of an army example is visible at Corbridge (*Corstopitum*) on Hadrian's Wall.

The Roman state imposed its own religion on the native Britons in the form of classical style temples administered by colleges of priests maintained at the expense of the public. In contrast to the earlier Greek examples, Roman temples (Fig.228.) were set on podiums, or high platforms, reached via a flight of steps. Rows of freestanding columns held up a triangular pediment forming a porch, leading to a *cella*, or shrine, which held a cult statue.

While such sites are rare in Britain, there are examples at Colchester and Bath. Romano-British temples did not involve congregations, as worship took place in the open area around an altar. The commonest kind of temple was the so-called Romano-Celtic type, with the *cella* forming a squat tower with a surrounding veranda, the plan forming two concentric squares. A good reconstruction of one of these types of temple can be seen in Buxton Museum. There are other patterns including polygonal and circular styles, and occasionally walls replaced the pillared veranda. Celtic divinities were of purely local significance, and inscriptions relating to them can be seen in a number of museums.

Temples hallowed to Oriental deities are known in Britain, and include those dedicated to Mithras, Serapis (Fig.229.), Isis and so on. They usually have an apsed plan form, with a nave and aisles, and were designed for small groups of worshippers. They are similar to Christian churches, and although some have been located, only the one at Colchester can be seen today.

Fig.228. The little apsed temple at Benwell on Hadrian's Wall was dedicated to the Tyne river god Antenociticus, but was a model for many small buildings of similar type throughout Roman Britain.

Fig.229. There were a number of temples dedicated to foreign deities, such as the one at York (Eboracum), which was built for the Egyptian god Serapis by the Legate (Commanding Officer) of the VI Legion.

Fig.230. *Many military and civilian tombstones survive in the province. This example in York was erected in memory of Lucius Duccius Rufinus, a signifer (standard bearer) of the IX Legion. Lucius, who died at the age of 28, holds the standard in his right hand.*

Fig.231. *An elaborate tombstone from the fort at Templeborough, Rotherham, in memory of an auxiliary, Cintismus, soldier of the 4th Cohort of Gauls. The stone had been reused as a drain cover later in the fort's history, and is now in the town museum.*

A variety of tombstones, both military and civilian, often with relief sculpturing, can be viewed in most major museums, and their inscriptions are both interesting and revealing. The military examples are dedicated both to infantry and cavalry (Figs.230-234.) Civilian ones include details of trades, professions and origins (Fig.235.), and are of immense value to historians. Cemeteries (Figs.236&237.) were usually situated outside town and city walls, a legal requirement by the authorities, and were placed alongside the main roads for the attention of wayfarers. A few large tombs, including *sarcophagi* (Fig.238.) and *mausolea* have survived, and can be seen either in situ, or in museums such as York (*Eboracum*). Other stonework includes inscriptions, of which a vast number survive (Fig.239&240.), statuary (Fig.241), and altars dedicated to a variety of deities (Fig.242.).

Fig.233.

Fig.234.

Fig.232. *The famous tombstone of Longinus Sdadapeze from Colchester, a duplicarius of the 1st cavalry regiment of Thracians. Amazingly, the broken-off face of the horseman was found in 1996 in the same place where the memorial was discovered in 1928. Longinus is shown riding down an enemy of villainous appearance, symbolising victory over death.*

Fig.233. *Another fine equestrian tombstone is this one dedicated to Rufus Sita at Gloucester. He was a trooper of the 6th Cohort of Thracians, and died aged 40, after 22 years' service. In this depiction, the trooper is spearing another armed but supine adversary.*

Fig.234. *The tombstone of Sextus Valerius Genialis from Cirencester. He was a Frisian who served in a turma (troop) of Thracians. Again a recalcitrant foe is being trampled and despatched with the spear.*

Fig.235.

Fig.235. In Ilkley Museum is this once imposing tombstone to an unknown girl of the Cornovian tribe, perhaps the companion of one of the auxiliaries serving in the fort, and who died at the age of 30. Note her long plaits, and the high-backed armchair she occupies. The stone was later modified for another purpose by carving away the sides.

Fig.237. Another inhumation cemetery at York, showing extended skeletons with pots containing food offerings placed at their knees. Note how one burial in the centre of the plate has partly destroyed a body placed immediately below. The interments are criss-crossed in no apparent order.

Fig.236. An extramural cemetery at Trentham Gardens, York, showing inhumation burials accompanied by a variety of pottery vessels.

Fig.238. Large and expensive sarcophagi such as this example from York were fashioned for very rich clients. This one is dedicated to the memory of Julia Fortunata from Sardinia, a loyal wife to her husband, Verecundius Diogenes.

Fig.239. This inscription, from the fort at Brough (Navio), Derbyshire, and now in Buxton Museum, records the reoccupation of the site by the 1st Cohort of Aquitanians under Julius Verus, during the reign of Emperor Antoninus, around the year AD 158.

Fig.240. Another dedicatory inscription at Buxton comes from the fort at Melandra Castle (Ardotalia) and commemorates the completion of building work by a century of the 1st Cohort of Frisiavones under Valerius Vitalis.

Fig.241. Statue of a young child, possibly part of a funerary monument, and exhibited in Sheffield City Museum.

Fig.242. A good example of a dedicatory altar found on the site of the vicus belonging to the fort at Brough, Derbyshire, and dedicated to Hercules Augustus by the fort's commandant, Proculus. It is now in Sheffield City Museum.

Fig.243. Fine Roman tableware included this selection of samian vessels, imported from Gaul, and available until the end of the 2nd century. A variety of designs and potter's stamps enable experts to closely date the products of these famous kilns.

Fig.244. A samian bowl from Aldborough, showing the Classical motifs in relief decoration embossed on this kind of pottery, including a depiction of Hercules battling with a lion and seen on the right.

One of the great Romano-British industries was pottery. This ranged from crude locally-produced wares, to refined types of ceramic, made both in Britain or imported from the continent. Among the finest ceramics was the so-called samian ware, a rich red pottery exported from Gaul, and embellished with fine relief decoration (Figs.243&244.).

Other choice vessels were made in the south-east like the Colchester vase, with its scenes of gladiatorial combat (Fig.245.). Military and civilian styles included *mortaria* or mixing bowls and jugs (Figs.246&247.), while other "kitchen" wares comprised strainers and dishes (Fig.248.). Fig.249 shows samples of "native" wares made by British potters. Some vessels were utilised for burial, and contained cremations (Figs.250&251).

Fig.245. The Colchester vase is another fine locally-produced beaker, with the figures of battling gladiators forming the decoration. The contestants are named, and would have been familiar figures to contemporary citizens.

Fig.245.

Fig.246. A selection of pottery which includes a mortarium (mixing-bowl) at lower right, embellished with a potter's stamp. Other items include a lamp, a samian bowl, and a pitcher.

Fig.247. Derby Museum's displays of Roman artefacts include two mortaria, one stamped, at the bottom of the photograph, a samian bowl, and two locally-produced pots. The smallest of the pair is a Derbyshire ware jar of the sort made at the nearby Hazelwood potteries and widely distributed throughout the province.

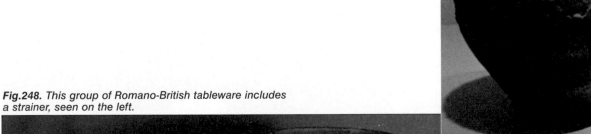

Fig.248. This group of Romano-British tableware includes a strainer, seen on the left.

Fig.249. A variety of ceramics from Aldborough includes jars, jugs, water or wine vessels, bowls and rusticated ware, whose surfaces have been deliberately roughened by the maker to prevent them slipping out of wet or greasy hands.

Fig.250. These jars from the Roman fort at Slack, Huddersfield, were used to hold cremations, and were unearthed in the cemetery adjoining the site.

Fig.251. Found in a cemetery at York, this cremation urn was accompanied with a small beaker and a faceted and handled glass bottle.

Fig.252. Fine glassware was available to those Romano-Britons rich enough to afford it. These superbly made and delicately coloured bowls and jugs were imported from the Rhineland.

Fig.253. A blue glass jug found in York, again accompanying a burial in one of the city's many cemeteries.

Glassware was likewise imported from the Rhineland, like the elegant and delicately coloured examples shown in Fig.252. More utilitarian glass containers included squat jugs such as the one shown in Fig.253. Superb jewellery was produced by native artificers, and included a variety of brooches, rings and other forms. (Fig.254.). Diminutive metal statues of the various gods and goddesses of the Empire were produced on a large scale, for household shrines, and are not uncommon finds on Romano-British sites (Figs.255&256.).

Fig.254. A notable assemblage of Roman jewellery, including cruciform and trumpet brooches on the right, penannular brooches and rings at the top, and hairpins, a silver ring, and a gold earring on the left.

Fig.255. Small statues like this bronze one of Jupiter were doubtless placed in household shrines by devotees of this god.

Fig.256. Another diminutive bronze statue, this time of Mercury, and again probably intended for display in the home or temple.

Fig.254.

Fig.255.

Fig.256.

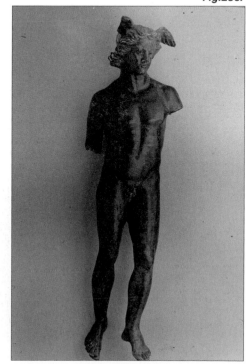

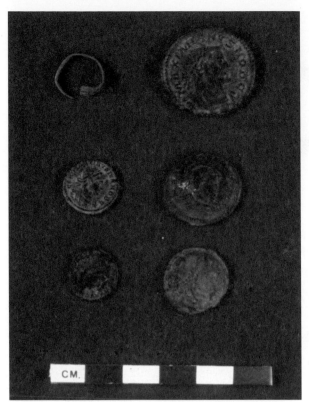

Fig.257. Huge numbers of coins were retailed during the course of the Roman occupation of Britain, and are a study in themselves. These bronze specimens were small change lost by local shepherds on a Derbyshire site.

Vast numbers of coins were retailed during the Roman occupation (Fig.257.), and the best modern study of these artefacts can be found in Adrian Marsden's **Roman Coins Found In Britain**, published by Greenlight in 2001.

One great industry during the period was lead mining, in Derbyshire, Yorkshire and the Mendips, and stray lead pigs, lost en route for export, are not uncommon finds. A cache of these lead bars was found in a warehouse at the Yorkshire port of Brough (*Petuaria*), and two of them are on display at Hull Museum (Fig.258.).

Other occasional finds are the milestones set up alongside Roman roads in Britain (Fig.259-260.). Very rarely these still remain in situ, as at Chesterholm along the Stanegate road, which ran south of Hadrian's Wall.

Fig.258. Lead was one of the more important Romano-British industries. This cast pig from Derbyshire was sent to Brough-on-Humber for shipment abroad, but got no further than the warehouse. The cast lettering indicates that it came from the Lutudarum lead works near Carsington. It is displayed in the Hull and East Riding Museum.

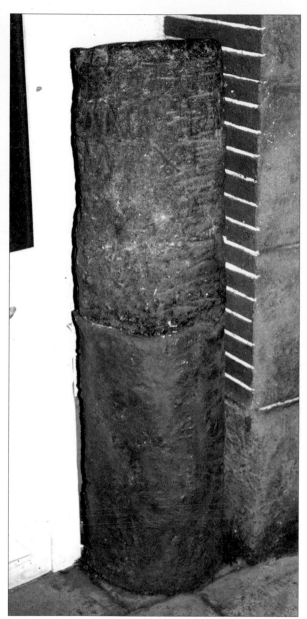

Fig.259. Several milestones are on display in various museums, including this example in Buxton Museum. The inscription indicates the distance to the nearby fort at Brough.

Fig.260. This uninscribed example stands in its original position on the Stanegate Road at Chesterholm just south of Hadrian's Wall.

Fig.261. *The massive wall of the Saxon Shore fortress of Burgh Castle (Branodunum) west of Great Yarmouth in Norfolk. The walls are still in good condition despite the robbing-out of their facing stones.*

Following the death of Emperor Severus in York in 211, Roman Britain enjoyed a lengthy period of security and consolidation. A growing prosperity in the countryside is evidenced by the building of new villas and the restructuring of others, often with lavish mosaics. However, the coasts became more and more susceptible to incursions by raiding parties (consisting of ancestors of the Saxons) from across the North Sea. These led to the building of a chain of coastal forts - the "Saxon Shore" - from Norfolk round to Portsmouth, garrisoned by marines who were geared to meet the enemy at sea.

Good examples of these fortresses can be seen at *Branodunum* (Fig.261.) west of Great Yarmouth, at Pevensey (*Anderida*) (Fig.262.) in Sussex, and Portchester (*Portus Adurni*) near Portsmouth (Fig.263.) in Hampshire. In 286 the commander of the Channel Fleet, Carausius, who had successfully checked the pirates, declared himself the ruler of Britain and the adjacent part of Gaul. Although killed off by his deputy Allectus in 293, this short episode showed how easy it was for remote provinces to be lost.

Fig.262. The even more imposing walls at the fortress of Pevensey (Anderida), still nearly 6m high, and embodying solid bastions for artillery emplacement. In medieval times the defences were utilised for a castle. It was even refortified in 1940 as a strongpoint in the event of a German invasion.

Fig.263. Portchester (Portus Adurni) near Portsmouth, still retains its walls and bastions, plus the V-ditch visible in the photograph. Like Pevensey its fortifications were adapted into a medieval castle.

Fig.264. *At the beginning of the 4th century Constantine rebuilt the defences of the Legionary Fortress at York, which included a series of massive polygonal towers fronting the River Ouse. Only the north-western multangular tower survives, although the upper layers are medieval.*

Severus had divided Britannia into two provinces: *Superior*, the nearest to Rome; and *Inferior*, the latter with York (Figs.264&265.) as its capital. In 284 Emperor Diocletian further subdivided Britain into four, forming the *Diocese* of Britain, which became part of the *Prefecture* of the Gauls. A fifth province of Britain was added in 369.

The early 4th century saw the arrival of a further wave of villas, new ones in the north and restructured examples in the south. The resulting large estates were able to outlast a time of huge inflation and social hardship, which forced many smallholders

Fig.265. *Alongside the multangular tower is a good stretch of contemporary wall, which is illustrated here. The back of this wall contains rough and un-smoothed masonry, as the stonework was covered by an earthen rampart.*

and peasants into bondage or even slavery. On the surface, however, all seemed well and Britain still looked a good investment to foreign speculators.

There had been occasional troubles on the northern frontier of Roman Britain for 50 years, but matters came to a head in 367 with the great "Barbarian Conspiracy" when the Picts from Scotland, the Scots from Ireland and the Saxons united to overrun the province. Hadrian's Wall was lost, and Count Theodosius was sent to recover the ravaged territory. It took two years before Britain was once again rescued.

Fig.266. Another town that added bastions to its already formidable walls was Caerwent in Monmouthshire. Though strictly in Wales, the defences here are carbon copies of those erected around Roman towns in England.

Fig.267. The still upstanding walls at Chester (Deva) had turrets added to its walls, as this example shows. As at York, the upper courses of masonry forming the city walls are medieval.

It is uncertain how far the towns and villas of Lowland Britain were affected after this setback, but Theodosius's reconstruction seems to have been successful, judging by the ongoing prosperity of the towns and villas until the end of the century. However, unrest in the countryside was on the increase, and the towns became fortified strongholds, with wider, deeper ditches and bastions added to the walls (Figs.266&267.). Urban self-defence was increased with the hiring of mercenaries of Germanic extraction. This policy eventually provided the groundwork for full Saxon settlement after the final breaking of the Roman links in 410.

Coastal defences were improved with the construction of the Yorkshire signal stations in the 370s (Fig.268.), while the frontier was manned by a peasant militia. By 407 the regular Roman forces were withdrawn, and in 410 Emperor Honorius told the quondam province to look to its own defence. A 360-year era had come to an end, and Britannia was abandoned to its fate.

Fig.268. *The latest military buildings were the Yorkshire signal stations erected by Count Theodosius in the 370s to give warning of seaborne attacks by Saxon pirates. This artist's impression shows the main components of the defences, which included a tall, square tower, plus a bastioned wall and ditch.*

A number of English museums contain material from the Romano-British era, and the main ones are mentioned in the following paragraphs. In the far north, the Hadrian's Wall district is well represented. From east to west, the enthusiast can begin with the Museum of Antiquities of the University of Newcastle on Tyne, with its excellent representation of the Mithraeum at Carrawburgh. At Chesters (*Cilurnum*), is the superb little museum purpose-built in the 19th century by the owner and excavator of the site, John Clayton. Further west the supply base at Corbridge (*Corstopitum*) has an excellent site museum, as does the fort at Housesteads (*Vercovicium*). The fort and township at nearby Chesterholm (*Vindolanda*) also boasts a very good collection; further sites include the museum at the Birdoswald (*Camboglanna*) fort, and the Roman Army Museum at Carvoran. Finally the museum at Carlisle includes a wealth of local Roman material.

In Yorkshire, the Hull and East Riding Museum houses some interesting mosaics and painted wall plaster from local sites, plus other artefacts, while York itself has an exemplary assemblage from the Roman city. Doncaster (*Danum*) Museum has a valuable collection, while the Roman town of Aldborough (*Isurium*) has a small but significant museum on site, as has Malton (*Derventio*) where there are the remnants of a Roman fort. The museum at Rotherham displays artefacts from the nearby fort at Templeborough, and other local sites, and includes some fine tombstones. There is a good Roman museum at Chester (*Deva*), another at Wroxeter (*Viroconium*), while Derby (*Derventio*) Museum houses a worthwhile display from the fort, associated settlement, and nearby potteries. The small but engaging little museum at Buxton (*Aquae Arnemetiae*) has a reconstruction of a Romano-Celtic temple, plus material from the town and nearby

forts. At Wall (*Letocetum*) in Staffordshire, a small museum houses some notable Celtic sculptures. The Jewry Wall Museum at Leicester (*Ratae*), as well as preserving part of the public bathhouse wall, holds some choice mosaics and wall plaster, and Lincoln (*Lindum*) likewise has its treasures from this period.

In the south-west, Gloucester (*Glevum*) Museum has a length of the city wall, and some notable sculptures, while the Corinium Museum in Cirencester is one of the finest in England, with reconstructed rooms and a small Roman garden. At Bath (*Aqua Sulis*) is the splendid Roman Bath Museum, with its associated complex of structures relating to the great religious and health centre. Dorchester (*Durnovaria*), boasts an amphitheatre (Maumbury Rings), a 4th century Roman town house, with a mosaic, plus other mosaics and artefacts in the museum.

North of London, the St Albans (*Verulamium*) Museum likewise houses a select display from the Roman city.

The British Museum obviously has some material of national importance, including the outstanding mosaic from Hinton St Mary in Dorset, while the London Museum holds artefacts from the city itself.

The Colchester and Essex Museum has displays, which trace the evolution of the settlement from fortress to full *colonia*. Canterbury (*Durovernum*) has excellent Roman collections in the city museum, and walls and mosaics from a town house in Butchery Lane. Dover (*Dubris*) has the fine remains of the so-called "Painted House", its standing walls embellished with painted plaster, and hypocausts under the floors. Chichester (*Noviomagus*) houses material from the Roman settlement there, and the nearby Roman Fishbourne Palace displays mosaics from other sites in Sussex, as well as those found in the luxury villa itself.

Museums
To Visit

The following list of museums hold collections relevant to the subject matter of this book.

ALDBOROUGH
Aldborough Roman Town & Museum
Main Street, Aldborough, S Yorks YO5 9EF
Tel: 01423 322768

AVEBURY
Alexander Keiller Museum
High Street, Avebury, Wiltshire SN8 1RF
Tel: 01672 539250
Email: wavgen@smtp.ntrust.org.uk

BATH
Roman Baths
Pump Room, Stall Street, Bath, Somerset BA1 1LZ
Tel: 01225 477785
Email: romanbaths_bookings@bathnes.gov.uk
Web: www.romanbaths.co.uk

BRISTOL
Bristol City Museum & Art Gallery
Queens Road, Bristol, Somerset BS8 1RL
Tel: 0117 922 3571
Web: www.bristol-city.gov.uk/museums

BUXTON
Buxton Museum & Art Gallery
Terrace Road, Buxton, Derbyshire SK17 6DA
Tel: 01298 24658

CARLISLE
Tullie House Museum & Art Gallery
Castle Street, Carlisle, Cumbria CA3 8TP
Tel: 01228 534781
Email: enquiries@tullie-house.co.uk
Web: www.tulliehouse.co.uk

CHELTENHAM
Cheltenham Art Gallery & Museum
Clarence Street, Cheltenham,
Gloucestershire GL50 3JT
Tel: 01242 237431
Email: artgallery@cheltenham.gov.uk
Web: www.cheltenhammuseum.org.uk

CHESTER
Grosvenor Museum
27 Grosvenor St, Chester, Cheshire CH1 2DD
Tel: 01244 402008
Email: s.rogers@chestercc.gov.uk
Web: www.chestercc.gov.uk/heritage/museum/home.html

CHOLLERFORD
Chesters Fort & Museum
Chollerford, Humshaugh, Hexham-on-Tyne,
Northumbria NE46 4EP
Tel: 01434 681379

CIRENCESTER
Corinium Museum
Park Street, Cirencester, Gloucestershire GL7 2BX
Tel: 01285 655611
Email: simone.clark@cotswold.gov.uk
Web: www.cotswold.gov.uk

COLCHESTER
Castle Museum
Castle Park, Colchester, Essex CO1 1TJ
Tel: 01206 282939
Web: www.colchestermuseums.org.uk

CORBRIDGE
Corbridge Roman Site Museum
Corbridge, Northumberland NE45 5NT
Tel: 01434 632349

DERBY
Derby Museum & Art Gallery
The Strand, Derby, Derbyshire DE1 1BS
Tel: 01332 716659
Web: www.derby.gov.uk/museums

DEVIZES
Wiltshire Heritage Museum
41 Long Street, Devizes, Wiltshire SN10 1NS
Tel: 01380 727369
Email: wanhs@wiltshireheritage.org.uk
Web: www. wiltshireheritage.org.uk

DORCHESTER
Dorset County Museum
High West Street, Dorchester, Dorset DT1 1XA
Tel: 01305 262735

HAYDON BRIDGE
Housteads Roman Fort & Museum
Haydon Bridge, Northumbria NE47 6NN
Tel: 01434 344363

HEXHAM
Chesterholm Museum - Vindolanda
Bardon Mill, Hexham, Northumbria NE47 7JN
Tel: 01434 344277
Email: info@vindolanda.com
Web: www.vindolanda.com

HUDDERSFIELD
Tolson Memorial Museum
Wakefield Road, Huddersfield, W. Yorks HD5 8DJ
Tel: 01484 223830
Web: www.kirkleesmc.gov.uk

ILKLEY
Manor House Art Gallery & Museum
Castle Yard, Ilkley, W. Yorks LS29 9DT
Tel: 01943 600066

KINGSTON-ON-HULL
Hull & East Riding Museum
36 High Street, Hull, Humberside
Tel: 01482 613902
Email: museums@hullcc.gov.uk
Web: www.hullcc.gov.uk/museums

LEICESTER
Jewry Wall Museum
St Nicholas Circle, Leicester,
Leicestershire LE1 4LB
Tel: 0116 247 3021
Web: www.leicestermuseums.ac.uk

LINCOLN
Greyfriars
Broadgate, Lincoln, Lincolnshire LN2 1HQ
Tel: 01522 530401
Email: hollandk@Lincolnshire.gov.uk

LONDON
British Museum
Great Russell Street, London WC1B 3DG
Tel: 020 7323 8000
Email: information@thebritishmuseum.ac.uk
Web: www.thebritishmuseum.ac.uk

Museum of London
150 London Wall, London EC2Y 5HN
Tel: 020 7600 3699
Email: info@museumoflondon.org.uk
Web: www.museumoflondon.org.uk

MALTON
Malton Museum
Market Place, Malton, N. Yorks YO17 7LP
Tel: 01635 695136

MANCHESTER
The Manchester Museum
The University of Manchester, Oxford Road,
Manchester M13 9PL
Tel: 0161 275 2634

NEWCASTLE UPON TYNE
Museum of Antiquities
University of Newcastle upon Tyne,
Newcastle upon Tyne NE1 7RU
Tel: 0191 222 7849
Email: l.allason-jones@ncl.ac.uk
Web: www.ncl.ac.uk/antiquities

NEWPORT
Roman Legionary Museum
High Street, Caerleon, Newport,
S. Wales NP18 1AE
Tel: 01633 423134
Email: www.nmgw.ac.uk

OXFORD
Ashmolean Museum of Art & Archaeology
Beaumont Street, Oxford OX1 2PH
Tel: 01865 278000
Web: www.ashmol.ox.ac.uk

PETERBOROUGH
Flag Fen Bronze Age Centre
The Droveway, Northey Road
Peterborough PE6 7QJ
Tel: 01733 313414
Email: info@flagfen.com

PRESTON
Ribchester Roman Museum
Riverside, Ribchester, Preston PR3 3XS
Tel: 01254 878261

SALISBURY
Salisbury & South Wiltshire Museum
The King's House, 65 The Close, Salisbury SP1 2EN
Tel: 01722 332151
Email: museum@salisburymuseum.freeserve.co.uk
Web: www.salisburymuseum.org.uk

SCARBOROUGH
Rotunda Museum of Archaeology & Local History
Museum Terrace, Vernon Road, Scarborough,
N. Yorks YO11 2NN
Tel: 01723 232323

SHEFFIELD
Sheffield City Museum
Western Park, Western Bank, Sheffield,
S. Yorks S10 2TP
Tel: 0114 278 2600
Email: info@sheffieldgalleries.org.uk
Web: www. sheffieldgalleries.org.uk

SHREWSBURY
Wroxeter Roman City
Wroxeter Roman Site, Wroxeter, Shrewsbury,
Shropshire SY5 6PH
Tel: 01743 761330

SKIPTON
The Craven Museum, Skipton Town Hall,
Skipton, N. Yorks.
Tel: 01756 706407

SOUTH SHIELDS
Arbeia Roman Fort & Museum
Baring Street, South Shields,
Tyne & Wear NE33 2BB
Tel: 0191 456 1369
Web: www.twmuseum.org.uk

ST ALBANS
Verulamium Museum
St Michaels, St Albans, Hertfordshire AL3 4SW
Tel: 01727 751810
Email: a.coles@stalbans.gov.uk
Web: www.stalbansmuseums.org.uk

TORQUAY
Torquay Museum
529 Babbacombe Road, Torquay, Devon TQ1 1HG
Tel: 01803 293975

WHITBY
Whitby Museum
Pannett Park, Whitby, N. Yorks YO21 1RE
Tel: 01947 602908
Email: graham@durain.demon.co.uk
Web: www.whitby-museum.org.uk

WOODSTOCK
Oxfordshire Museum
Fletchers House, Park Street, Woodstock,
Oxfordshire OX20 1SN
Tel: 01993 811456
Email: oxonmuseum@oxfordshire.gov.uk
Web: www.oxfordshire.gov.uk

YORK
Yorkshire Museum
Museum Gardens, York, N. Yorks YO1 7FR
Tel: 01904 551800
Email: yorkshire.museum@york.gov.uk
Web: www.york.gov.uk/heritage/museums/yorkshire

Select Bibliography

Prehistoric Monuments

Burl, A.	**The Stone Circles of Britain, Ireland and Brittany**	Yale, 2000.
Darvil, T.	**Prehistoric Britain**	Routledge, 1987.
Dyer, J.	**Ancient Britain**	Routledge, 1997.
Dyer, J.	**Discovering Prehistoric England**	Shire, 2001.
Parker Pearson, M.	**Bronze Age Britain**	Routledge, 1993.
Pollard, J.	**Neolithic Britain**	Shire, 1997.
Wymer, J.	**Mesolithic Britain**	Shire, 1991.

Most aspects of Prehistoric Britain are covered, subject-by-subject, in the comprehensive Shire Archaeology series. Each book has its own specialised booklist, and anyone with specific interests in the period is advised to consult the regular catalogues available by ringing Shire Publications on 01844 344301.

Roman Monuments

Frere, S.S.	**Britannia**	Routledge, 1978.
Johnson, S.	**Later Roman Britain**	Routledge, 1980.
Johnston, D.E.	**Discovering Roman Britain**	Shire, 2002.
	Ordnance Survey Map of Roman Britain	Fourth Edition, 1978.
Potter, T.W. and Johns, C.	**Roman Britain**	British Museum, 1992.
Salway, P.	**Roman Britain**	Oxford, 1981.
Todd, M.	**Roman Britain**	Fontana, 1985.
Webster, G.	**The Roman Invasion of Britain**	Batsford, 1981.

As with prehistoric Britain, Shire Publications publish a range of books on practically all aspects of the period, and readers are urged to check the catalogues for any subject that interests them. Those with an interest in Roman coins should consult Adrian Marsden's **Roman Coins Found In Britain** published by Greenlight in 2001.

Great Books From Greenligh

This exciting title is produced in full colour with over 450 Celtic and Roman artefacts beautifully illustrated in over 150 pages.
● Bronze & Iron Age Artefacts ● Fibula Brooches ● Plate, Crossbow & Early Saxon Brooches ● Buckles & Military Equipment ● Locks, Keys & Knife Handles ● Spoons, Cosmetic Grinders, Medical Implements & Seal Boxes ● Jewellery ● Cube Matrices, Lead Seals and Gaming Pieces ● Pottery & Bronze Utensils ● Steelyard Weights & Bronze Mounts ● Figurines & Votive Objects ● Chart of Roman Gods ● Select Bibliography ● Full price guide for every item in two grades of condition
A4, 152 pages, ISBN 1 8977 38 37 4

This exciting new book covers the period from the 6th to 11th centuries and - together with "Celtic & Roman Artefacts" and "Medieval Artefacts" (also by Nigel Mills) - completes the historical series covering artefacts from the Bronze Age to Tudor times. Illustrated in full colour and with over 250 superb photographs of individual objects, it encompasses the full spectrum of everyday items in use in Anglo-Saxon England in chronological sequence. The selection of illustrations has been built up over a period of 15 years from various collections. The objects covered include: buckles, strap ends, pins, cruciform brooches, disc brooches, animal brooches, jewellery, beads, stirrup mounts, wrist clasps, dress hooks, keys, knives, tweezers, weights, gaming counters, and weapons. There is also a Norse mythology genealogical chart of the gods. There are additional notes and advice for collectors. The book is an invaluable reference work for collectors, dealers, museums, and archaeologists. Full price guide for every item in two grades of condition.
A4, 108 pages, ISBN 1 8977 38 05 6

Medieval Artefacts, ... indispensible referenc. work, 116 pages, all colour, price guide, w. over 300 beautiful illustrations spaning t. period 1066-1500. Contents include: Introduction (Mudlark and Historical Background), Buckles, Strapends, Seal Matric. Thimbles, Pilgrim Bad. Finger Rings, Brooch Buckles, Buttons & Pin. Heraldic Pendants, Keys, Locks & Weights, Spoons, Knives Pottery, Gaming, Purses & Pa. Bullas, Sporting & Hunting (inc Spurs, Arrowheads, Daggers, Sword Pommels & Chapes), Figurines & Church Vessels. Full pr. guide for every item in two grades of conditio.
A4, 116 pages ISBN 1 8977 38 27 7

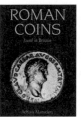

Roman coins were used in Britain for nearly 400 years and are common finds in the soil of this country. This book begins with a step-by-step guide to the identification of these fascinating objects and then discusses a range of other aspects relating to them, including a chapter on the often neglected 'barbarous' imitations. Numerous tables and lists, together with over 400 photographs make this book not only an invaluable guide for the beginner but also gathers together in one place a stock of information for easy reference. **The chapter titles are:** Introduction to Roman coins and their identification ● Coin legends and understanding the inscriptions on Roman coins ● Portraits and propaganda ● Mints: Differences between mints, mintmarks in the later empire ● Roman coins in the earlier empire, up to 238 ● The radiate coinages, 238-296 ● The fourth century ● The end of Roman coinage in Britain ● Contemporary forgeries in Roman Britain ● Treatment of coins, preservation, cataloguing etc. Full price guide in two grades of condition.
A4, 108 pages ISBN 1 8977 38 06 4

Buried British Treasure Hoards by Ted Fletcher, tells the fascinating stories of some of the most spectacular finds in a way designed to help you find the next hoard. Contents include: Golden Hoards From the Bronze Age, Celtic Buried Treasures, The Riches Of Roman Britain, Where Are Those Anglo-Saxon Treasures? The Romance Of Medieval Treasure Troves, Unearthing The Secrets Of The Civil War, Hiding & Discovering Hoards In Modern Times, Finders Sharers - Treasure Trove Laws, Choosing Your Tools.
A4 - 116 pages, ISBN 1 8977 38 12 9

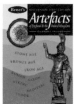

Benets is a detailed guide to Briti. antiquities. This publication from Valued History in Cambridge con. over 1,000 colour photos of objec. found in the British Isles. These from the Stone Age right through the post-Medieval period, and it comes complete with a price guid. Beautifully produced in hardback book contains 316 pages.
● Stone Age ● Bronze Age ● Celti. Iron Age ● Roman ● Anglo-Saxon ● Viking ● Norman, Medieval & Tudor ● Post Tudor
Benet's is not an academic study nor an archaeological report of objects discovered and this is reflected in the verbal descriptions. Benet's is, however, a visual guide identification purposes and to market prices. It is hope. that such a visual aid to identification will encourage finders in particular to undertake further research into class of item which they have found.
A5 - 300 pages, + £3 p&p

A new authoritative book compiled for collectors and those interested in the design of buttons. This book is an ideal reference work for identification of button finds. It contains 375 button examples reproduced in colour, including Livery and Royal Court buttons as well as General issues; there is also a chapter upon Button Making.
The chapter headings are:
1 - General Overview
2 - Differentiations & Updating
3 - Livery Buttons   4 - Royal Court Buttons
5 - Collecting Themes   6 - Button Making & Backmarks
Full price guide
A5 - 92 pages ISBN 1 8977 38 048

Buckles 1250-1800, written by Ross Whitehead, contains over 800 illustrated buckles, with full supporting description and background text. Also with 12 full colour plates. A unique classification format using shape rather than type or period, aids identification. Contents include; buckle manufacture, single looped buckles, buckles with integral plates, clasp fastners, annular buckles, rectangular and trapezoidal buckles, asymmetrical buckles, two piece buckles and finally buckles as jewellery. Full price guide.
A4 - 128 pages ISBN 1 8977 38 17x

This is the definitive referenc. work on English Groats. Writ. by Ivan Buck, it covers the gr. from its introduction in the re. of Edward I (1272-1307) righ. to the end of the Tudors in th. early 17th century. Essential reading - this work helps to identify the various types of g. and the major varieties.There over 400 colour illustrations i. the text and a number of scar. and rare coins are illustrated. the first time. In many cases the information provided. be applied to the parallel series of half groats.
A4 - 68 pages ISBN 1 8977 38 420

Metal Artefacts of Antiquity by Brian Read with over 950 archaeological quality illustrations this title is a great aid to identification and dating metal artefacts
Contents include: Mounts, Pendant Suspension Mounts and Pendants, Strap Distributors, Terrets, Spurs and Spur Fittings, Horses' Bit, Keys and Locks, Seal-Boxes, Seal Matrices; Daggers and Knives and their Fittings, Sword Fittings, Spear, Tools, Spoons, Brooches, Weights and Weighing Apparatus, Candleholders, Lamp Suspenders and Lanterns, Purse Bars and Pendent Frames, Lead Tokens.
Principal illustrator Patrick Read, additional illustrations by Nick Griffiths, foreword by Geoff Egan.
A4 148 pages ISBN 0 953245 020

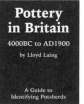

This book aims to provide an introductory guide to identifying some of the basic types of po. that may be found by accident, in systematic fieldwalking, and in archaeological excavation. Clay is an exceptionally versatile material. It can be made into many useful and beautiful objects, decorated in a splendid variety of ways, and, if exposed to high temperatures, made into pottery.
Although pottery is easily broken, the individual sherds are remarkably resilient. Sherds are therefore the most frequent types of find on archaeological sites and their presence in the s. can lead to the discovery of new sites. While many people can distinguish porcelain from earthenware, not everyone can tell the difference between stoneware and tin glaze or a Bror. Age urn from a modern flowerpot.
Since whole pots are very rare finds the emphasis is on sherds rather than museum or collectors' pieces.
The book deals mostly with pottery made in Britain, though at all times it must be borne in mind that any pottery found could have come from any period or any location in the world.
The book contains 178 illustrations, mainly in colour, and is divided into the following sections:
The potter's craft, The study of pottery, Prehistoric pottery- the Neolithic Period circa 4000-2000 BC, Prehistoric pottery - The Bronze Age circa 2000-700 BC, Prehistoric pottery - The Iron Age circa 700/600 BC-43 AD, Prehistor. pottery - The Iron Age circa 700/600 BC-43 AD, The Dark Ages & Early Medieval Period, The Medieval Period - 11. 15th Centuries, The 16th & 17th Centuries, The 18th & 19th Centuries, Glossary of terminology.

Greenlight Publishing, 119 Newland Street, Witham, Essex CM8 1WF ● **Tel:** 01376 5219C
e-mail: books@greenlightpublishing.co.uk ● **web:** www.greenlightpublishing.co.uk

☎ **01376 521900**